THE POCKET DARING BOOK FOR GIRLS:

ADVENTURES & PURSUITS

Praise for *The Daring Book for Girls*

'Gung-ho girly advice . . . the boys had their Dangerous book, now this one is for us'   *Good Housekeeping*

'I can't imagine not wanting to get stuck in to *The Daring Book for Girls*. It's an admirable project'   Jenny Diski, *Sunday Times*

'The authors mix inspiring tales of girls who made good . . . with a scrap bag of how-tos for girlish activities . . . *The Daring Book for Girls* keeps . . . practical knowledge from getting drowned in the techno-flow'   *The New York Times*

'We've had *The Dangerous Book for Boys* – now it's our turn. Refreshingly, it's not about lipstick tips, but pioneering women who inspire us'   *Glamour*

THE POCKET DARING BOOK FOR GIRLS:

ADVENTURES & PURSUITS

This book is a mix of much-loved chapters from the popular *The Daring Book for Girls*, plus new adventures and activities for readers to discover – all of which are perfect for the rambling days of summer or any season. With its fun, portable size and compelling contents, this book of Adventures & Pursuits is perfect for any girl on the go.

Daring Girl badges and other downloads available at
www.daringbookforgirls.com

HarperCollins*Publishers*

HarperCollins*Publishers*
77–85 Fulham Palace Road,
Hammersmith, London W6 8JB

www.harpercollins.co.uk

Published by HarperCollins*Publishers* 2008
1

First published in the US, in a slightly different edition
by HarperCollins*Publishers* 2008

A catalogue record for this book
is available from the British Library

ISBN: 978–0–00–728803–8

Set in Minion by Newgen Imaging Systems (P) Ltd, Chennai, India

Printed and bound in Italy by L.E.G.O. SpA – Vicenza

Andrea Buchanan and Miriam Peskowitz

The Pocket
DARING
Book
for
Girls
Adventures & Pursuits

HarperCollins*Publishers*

CONTENTS

◆

INTRODUCTION

W E LOVE BOOKS. Fancy books, heavy books, books with gilded pages – you name it. But fancy books, impressive as they may be, aren't always practical to read on the go. This pocket book – small enough to fit in a backpack or beachbag – lends itself much better to adventuring. So we took our favourite activities from the original *The Daring Book for Girls* and assembled them into this pocket-sized edition of Adventures & Pursuits. Plus we added lots of new chapters we just know girls (and probably some boys, too) will love – wait until you read about making a zip line and skateboarding!

We hope you enjoy this collection of old and new favourites as you celebrate the Daring Girl credo: Enjoy yourself. Explore new things. Lead an interesting life.

Bon Voyage!

Andrea Buchanan
Miriam Peskowitz

CAMPING OUTDOORS

A QUICK TENT can be made with just a rope, some stakes and two tarpaulins – big plastic, waterproof sheets essential to camping. First, string a rope between two branches on two different trees. Then stretch one tarpaulin out on the ground and hang the second over the rope. Lastly, stake the four corners of the hanging tarpaulin to the ground, using a hammer or a rock.

Shop-bought tents are much larger than ever before, and come with flexible poles that fold into short lengths and stow away in a bag, making tent-pitching relatively simple. They also better protect us from the number one evil scourge of camping: insects. (The number two evil scourge, should you ask, is nettles.) This leads to the prime rule of tents: Keep the zip shut, because it's nearly impossible to shoo a mosquito out of your tent once it's in.

Before you pitch your tent, you may want to lay down an additional tarp to keep things extra clean and dry. (If you do, tuck the edges under so the tarp is slightly smaller than your tent.) Then set out the tent and follow directions for inserting the poles. The fly, which protects from rain and dew, goes over the top of the tent and usually clips on, is staked to the ground, or both. Finally, bang the tent pegs into the ground, lest large gusts of wind send your tent soaring towards Kansas.

You've just made your home outdoors. Here are the basic furnishings:

* The sleeping bag. To make things a bit more comfortable, add a sleeping pad underneath and bring along a pillow or just a pillow case you can stuff with clothes. Sleeping pads have become softer, longer and more elaborate, and can even involve air pumps, which your parents will undoubtedly appreciate if you invite them to sleep out with you.

* Torch and insect spray. Enough said.

* A coolbox. Filled with lots of drinking water and camping food staples like fresh apples and dried fruit.

Marshmallows are a necessity, too, if a campfire's involved.

The anti-litter mantra for sleeping and camping outdoors is: take it in, take it out. Since there are no bins in the wilderness, bring a bag for your wrappers and other rubbish.

Once you've learned to pitch a tent and roll out the sleeping bag in your garden, you can graduate to the full-on camping experience where the fridge and indoor toilet are not close at hand.

Camping is gear-intensive and takes careful planning, especially if you're hiking a few miles out. You must carry several days' food and water in your backpack, not to mention a camping stove and mess kit, soap and a toothbrush and so much more. When you're ready for a first experience at a wilderness campsite, find a friend whose family are pros, and learn from them.

Whether you are in your garden or the wildest part of the Pennines, remember the whole point of sleeping outdoors is to breathe in the night air, listen to nature's songs and drift off to sleep under the stars.

MAKE YOUR OWN ZIP LINE

❖

IF YOU CAN'T globe-trot to Costa Rica and ride a zip line in full harness above the rainforest canopy, you can build a more modest zip line in your own backgarden. Ours is simpler than a high-pressure steel cable stretched over 100 metres high in the air and uses a make-your-own grab bar and easily available rope.

You will need

* Twelve metal coat hangers (more if they're thin)
* Wide electrical tape and duct tape
* Lots of polyethylene rope (aka clothesline)
* Pulley, sized to match the rope, and strong enough to hold your weight
* Tape measure

Optional

* One or two eyebolts, with nuts and washers
* Enough wooden planks (about 5 centimetres × 25 centimetres) to make a ladder up your tree, a hammer and galvanized nails

Building a zip line in your backgarden presents a series of challenges to solve.

1. Where will the zip line start and stop?

Find a jumping-off spot and a landing spot: two trees, a tree house, a swing set, the edge of an elevated patio or deck. You can jump from the roof of a shed or a tree in your neighbour's garden. Consider how tall you and your friends are, how high up in the air you want to be and for how long. The zip line's starting point must be higher than the finishing point. Consider, too, the length of your line: too short and it's too quick a ride, but too long and it grinds to a stop, leaving you suspended in midair.

2. How will you climb to the starting point?
If the starting point is a tree, does it have low branches to climb? If not, find a ladder and wrap it against the tree, or hammer some wood planks into the trunk for footing. Galvanized nails are key because they won't rust and weaken.

3. How will you connect the rope to your starting point?
Once you've found your start and finish, measure the distance between them and triple or quadruple the number, since you'll need to wrap the line many times around the tree and tie it with a solid knot and it's much easier to cut off extra rope than to discover you don't have enough. Wrap the rope five or six times around the tree at the height you've chosen. End with a tautline hitch – see the chapter on Knots and Stitches. Double it if you want to be extra sure.

However, according to our tree experts, it's not so great to permanently wrap ropes around trees because it scars the bark and cuts off circulation. Believe it or not, it's better to knock a nail or bolt through a tree. For this option, find an eyebolt large enough for the rope and matched to the width of the tree, drill a large enough hole and secure it with a nut, washers on both sides. Knot the rope to the bolt.

4. What's the best grab bar to use?

The grab bar needs to be secure enough that it won't disintegrate when you're holding on for dear life and soft enough to hold comfortably with your hands as you whir through the air. Take your twelve metal hangers and undo the twist at the top of each one. Plait or weave the hangers together as best you can, to form a thick metal rope. Wrap the plaited metal with several layers of electrical wire but leave a few centimetres at each end unwrapped. The bottom of the pulley has an opening for an attachment. Insert one end of the grab bar through this hole. Then sculpt the hangers into a circular or oval shape and twist the strands together, one-to-one, to hold the circle tight. Wrap the whole contraption with electrical tape and then wrap it again. After that, cover many times with duct tape. The more tape, the better.

Now thread the zip line rope – already attached to the jumping off spot – through the pulley. Cut a smaller piece of rope that you can use to pull the grab bar back to the starting point and attach it to the grab bar. (By the way, once this system is up, you'll find many creative uses for pulleys. For instance, you might string a pulley system between your house and your friend's house next door and use clothespins or a basket to send messages, books, trading cards and borrowed clothing back and forth. The possibilities are endless.)

5. What is the slope and where is the endpoint?

The steeper the slope between the two trees, the faster the zip line will go and the more thrilling it will be. Leave enough give in the rope so the ride slows about three fourths of the way down. This will prevent you from slamming into a tree and wasting precious zip line time in Casualty. (Some kids drag an old mattress against the landing point to cushion the ending.) A one metre or one and a half metre difference in elevation between start and finish usually does the trick. Pull the rope tight at the ending point, wrap it many times around the tree and make a tautline hitch (or use an eyebolt here, too). You may have to experiment a few times with how high you tie the rope, rewrapping and tying several times until, by trial and error, the perfect amount of tension and slope is found.

SEVEN GAMES OF TAG

A GAME OF TAG can be as basic or as complicated as you like: you can revel in the pure straightforwardness of one person chasing another, or liven things up by adding rules and strategy. Either way, tag requires no equipment, no court, no uniform – just someone willing to be It, and others willing to run as fast as it takes to avoid getting tagged and becoming It themselves. Here are seven ways of playing tag.

1 **Chain/Chainey Tag.** In Chain Tag one person is It. But instead of being able to tag someone and no longer be It, the person who is It tags a player, and each player who is tagged then has to link arms with the tagger and join in as It. As more players are tagged, the link of taggers grows. No tags count if the chain separates. The game is over when the last player is finally tagged.

2 **Stuck in the Mud.** When a player is tagged in Stuck in the Mud, she must *freeze* in place immediately. Sometimes the game is played with the rule that other untagged players can *unfreeze* anyone who is frozen; the game can also be played so that the person who is It only wins when every single player is frozen.

3 **Shadow Tag.** This game is perfect towards the end of a sunny day when shadows are long, since the main rule of Shadow Tag is that whoever is It can tag a player by stepping on her shadow.

4 **Time Warp Tag.** This kind of tag is played just like normal tag, except that at any point during the game, any player (including whoever is It) can call out, 'Time Warp!' whereupon all players must move in slow motion. When 'Time Warp!' is called again, play returns to normal speed.

5 **Line Tag.** In Line Tag, which is played best on a playground or other surface with lines or painted areas on it, players are allowed to run or walk only on the lines. These can be hopscotch lines, netball court lines, or even lines on the pavement – if it's a line, you can step on it. Otherwise, you're out. If a player is tagged, she must sit down, and the only player who can move past her is the one who is It.

6 **Zombie Tag.** The person who is It must chase after the players 'zombie-style', staggering with her arms out in front of her and groaning like the undead. When the It zombie tags a player, that player also becomes a zombie. The game ends when all players have been transformed into moaning zombies.

7 **Hide and Seek Tag.** This is best played in woods with lots of places to hide. Everyone who is not It runs off while the seeker closes her eyes and counts to 100 next to a designated tree. The seeker calls, 'Ready or Not, Here I Come,' and begins searching for everyone else. The goal for those hiding is to get back to touch the tree before being tagged. Those who are tagged before touching the tree are also It and join the seeker. The last one to reach the tree or be tagged is the seeker in the next game.

HOW TO RUN FASTER

❖

EVER FELT LIKE the slowest runner in the group? Running faster is a combination of finding a longer stride in your steps; adding more strides per minute; gaining muscle strength in your legs, arms and torso; and visualizing yourself moving faster through the air. Here are things you can

practise so you can run like the wind, or at least fast enough to stay in the game!

Push off from the ball and toes of your back foot. Really jettison your body forwards and into the air. You'll feel the difference.

Lengthen your stride so your front leg extends to its full reach. If you aren't already leaning forwards just a little bit as you run, try that. To get a sense of how this should feel, find a hill and run down, as the hill automatically lengthens your stride.

Pump your arms, forwards and backwards, 'from pocket to jaw,' as the coaches say, with your elbows at a ninety-degree angle. The hands and arms should point in the direction you are running, which means your arms should neither cross in front of your body, nor flail out to the side. Relax your hands (no fists) and imagine holding a thin piece of paper between your thumb and third finger. Oh, and don't twist your chest and shoulders from side to side – only the arms move.

Try some interval training: jog for two minutes, sprint for thirty seconds, jog, sprint, jog, sprint. Or, near the end of a run, push yourself into a sprint. The sprint gets your body used to the extra effort of moving your legs faster and eventually, running faster will feel normal.

Pretend that you are quickstepping your way across a field of hot coals. Or run up a flight of stairs (but walk down). Both exercises get you used to lifting your feet off the ground quickly.

Time yourself, then try to beat your last time. Some adults use running logs to keep a record of how far and fast they run, to see evidence that they are getting faster. Be kind to yourself, though. It's just running.

BANDANA TYING

◆

THE WORD *BANDANA* has a global history. It comes from the Sanskrit *bhandhana,* which means tying. The word was absorbed first into Portuguese (in the sixteenth

century, Portugal had conquered the cities of Goa and Bombay, now called Mumbai, on the western coast of India). From Portuguese, the word entered English. We can thank Indian languages for an assortment of English clothing words, such as cashmere (from the northern

BANDANA TYING

region of Kashmir), cummerbund, bangle, khaki, pyjamas and dungarees.

Bandanas are often also called kerchiefs or headscarfs. A bandana can be a belt or a blindfold for Blind Man's Bluff. With a needle and thread, two or more can be sewn together to make a shirt or skirt.

You can wrap it loosely around your neck, cowboy style, pull it up over your nose and mouth for a disguise or use it to dress up your pet. Best of all, you can wrap treasures or lunch in a bandana, then attach it to a long stick and sling it over your shoulder when you head out to see the world.

Bandanas are an excellent way to cover your hair, too, while playing lacrosse or hiking on a hot day, and they make perfect headbands.

To tie a bandana around your head, fold it in half to make a triangle. Place the long edge on your forehead, however low or high you want (you'll most likely experiment with this, and try different possibilities). The cloth will fall lightly over your hair. With your hands, smooth it towards the back, push the tip of the triangle towards the nape of your neck. Then draw the ends over it, and tie (use your square knot from the chapter on Knots and Stitches).

You'll probably want to pull the triangle portion of the bandana into place, so it's smooth against your head, and so the corners don't stick out the sides.

If your head is larger, or if your mother or father wants to wear one, instead of folding the cloth in half, merely fold one corner towards the opposite corner, and go from there.

To turn a bandana into a headband, fold in half to make a triangle. Start folding in, from the tip of the triangle towards the long edge, till you're left with the size headband you want to wear. Wrap around your head and tie in the back.

BUILDING A CAMPFIRE

———◆———

SITTING AROUND A campfire is probably one of the oldest human activities. Nowadays, unless you're on a solo wilderness hike, a campfire is less a tool of survival than a social event – a chance to sing songs and tell stories and be out in the dark in nature with friends.

A fire needs three things: fuel, heat and air. The most common fuel is wood – main fuel such as logs cut from trees, and smaller fuel like tinder (twigs, strips of paper, or anything small that burns well) and kindling (branches and twigs about the size of a pencil and no thicker than a finger). Heat, which comes in the form of a flame or spark generated from matches, lighters, friction or even focused sunlight, should be generated from the smaller fuel, which will then ignite the larger fuel. And of course, fire needs oxygen, so make sure that your fuel is packed loosely enough to allow for air circulation. When there's not enough oxygen present, the fire goes out, which is why dousing flames with water or smothering a small fire with sand extinguishes the flames.

What you'll need to build your own campfire

* A fire ring, a fire pit, a fire pan, or other temporary fire site

* Water or sand to extinguish the fire

* Tinder

* Kindling

* Main fuel (thick, dry wood and logs – the thicker the wood, the longer the fire will burn)

* Matches or a lighter

BUILDING THE FIRE

The first item of business when building a fire is deciding where to make it. Find a spot away from tents, trees with low-hanging branches, or other flammable elements. Once you've determined your location, you can begin to assemble your fire. Ideally, you can use an existing fire pit or fire ring. If there isn't one handy, you can create a fire site yourself. One way is to clear away a space on the ground, dig a pit, line it with small rocks and then cover that area about half an inch deep with sand or aluminium foil. Otherwise you can use a fire pan, either a store-bought metal pan for the purpose of making fires, or any round metal surface, such as a pizza pan or a metal dustbin lid.

Once you have your site established, place your tinder (the small pieces you collected) in a small pile in the middle of the fire site. Around that, place the kindling, taking care not to pack it too tightly, as your fire will need air in order to burn. Arrange the kindling in a kind of 'teepee' format, as though you are creating a small tent around your tinder. Leave an opening so that you can light the tinder and keep some of your kindling in reserve, so you can add more to the fire as it takes hold.

Using a match, lighter, or your preferred method of ignition, light the tinder and gently fan or blow on it until it becomes a strong flame and ignites the kindling around it. Once the kindling is burning, you can add your main fuel – those large, thick logs that will burn long and bright. Add more kindling to the fire to keep it burning, but take care to keep the fire manageable. Also make sure to place your wood carefully and not just throw it onto the fire.

Once the fire is dwindling and it's time to put it out, use water to douse the flames completely. You can also use sand, if that is available, to smother the fire. Water is the most thorough method of putting out a fire and, when it comes to extinguishing fires, you definitely want to be thorough. Check to make sure there's nothing still smouldering, even when it seems like the fire is out. Everything – the fire site, the burned fuel, the area around the fire – should be cool to the touch before you leave. A fire that is carelessly put out, or not put out thoroughly enough, can flare up again.

MAKING A CLOTH-COVERED BOOK

———— ❖ ————

You will need

* Two pieces of 22 × 15.5 centimetre cardboard

* A needle or embroidery needle and thread

* Fabric (about 30 × 35 centimetres) – an old dress, T-shirt or pillowcase works well

* Eight pieces of A4 (21 × 29.5 centimetre) plain white paper (for a longer book, you can use more paper)

* 1 piece of fancy or coloured A4 (21 × 29.5 centimetre) paper

* Wide packing tape and regular tape

* A ruler

* Fabric glue

* 30-centimetre ribbon

* Scissors

Fold the plain paper and the fancy paper in half. If the fancy paper looks different on the front than it does on the back, fold it so that the 'front' side is on the inside. Put the folded plain paper inside the folded fancy paper, like a book. Then use your needle and thread to sew the papers together in two places, about 3 centimetres from the top and 3 centimetres from the bottom.

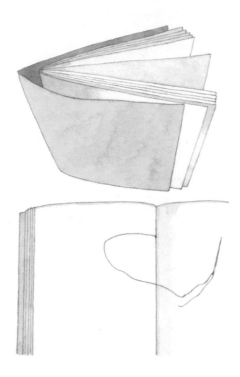

Cut your fabric to about 30 centimetres by 35 centimetres and lay it out, wrong side facing up. Place the two pieces of cardboard in the middle of the fabric, leaving about a centimetre between each piece. Tape the cardboard pieces together and maintain the centimetre separation. Coat the back of the cardboard lightly with fabric glue and then glue the cardboard to the cloth. Fold and glue each of the corners first and then fold and glue the fabric on each side. You can use tape to secure the fabric if necessary; just make sure the tape doesn't stick up close to the outer edge. Now you've made the fabric book cover.

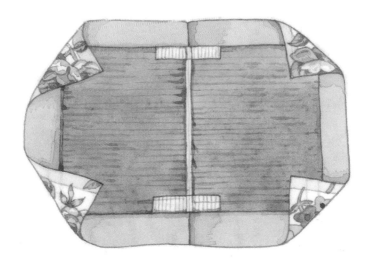

MAKING A CLOTH-COVERED BOOK

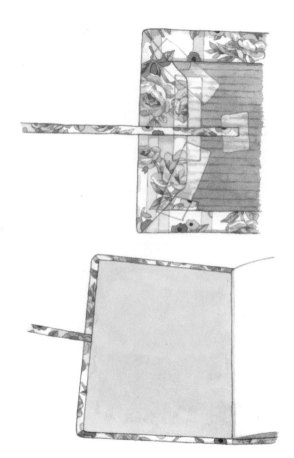

Cut your 30-centimetre ribbon in half. Use your ruler to find the centre of the left side of your fabric cover and glue the end of one ribbon there (starting about 5 centimetres from the end of the ribbon). Try not to overglue, but also try to make sure you glue right to the very edge so that the ribbon is firmly attached. Secure with tape. Do the same thing on the right side of the cover with the other ribbon.

MAKING A CLOTH-COVERED BOOK

Open your pages and place them in the middle of the cardboard and fabric so that the fold of the paper is right in the centre of the tape between the cardboard pieces. Using the fabric glue, glue the outer paper (the fancy paper) to the inside of the cover and let it dry. Once dry, tie the ribbon to close your book. It's not as secure as a lock and key, but it's a pretty way to keep safe your handmade journal, should you choose to use it as a secret diary.

HOW TO SKATEBOARD

Nose

Deck with grip tape

Bearing

Tail

Truck

Wheel

FIRST OF ALL, jump on the skateboard and find your stance. It might be regular, with your left foot forwards and your right foot at the back, ready to push. Or you might stand 'goofy', which simply means you prefer to push with your left foot, so that's at the back. One stance will feel more comfortable than the other and you can always change.

Skateboarding is all about change, confidence and believing in what you've started. Relax. Keep your knees loose and bent. Trust what your body can do. Wear some pads (elbows and knees and wrist guards). Use a helmet, no questions asked, one that covers the back of your head (a bike helmet doesn't really do the trick, but it's better than nothing). If skateboarding becomes your thing, skate shoes can be useful, because the bottoms are wider and flatter and have special strength in all the parts most likely to drag on the ground and wear out. Above all, to skateboard is to experiment, to have fun, to try new things. It's not about

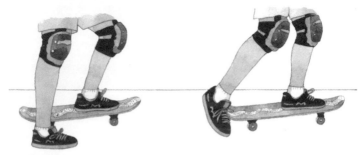

Feet forward

rules; it's about you and your vision of moving along the ground and through the air.

To push off: Your front toes and foot are over the front truck, your back foot pushes off the ground – a few times, most likely. Once the skateboard starts to roll, pull the back foot up to rest over the back truck. Both feet turn to face the side as you glide. To push off again, pivot your feet to face forwards. You will constantly shift from toes-facing-forwards to toes-facing-sideways and soon it will feel easy. You'll also learn to sway your hips, twist your shoulders and bend your knees to keep the board moving. That's on level ground. As soon as you start skateboarding downhill, you'll want some ways to stop. To foot break, face the front toes forward and put your weight on your front leg. Lower your back leg to the ground and drag it lightly along the ground, increasing the pressure until you stop. (Push too hard or too fast and you'll fall.) To heel drag, move the back heel off the tail of the skateboard, lean back until the nose of

Feet face side

the board pops into the air and grind the back heel into the ground. Of course, you can always jump! Crouch, jump and jog alongside as you land. If you jump forwards, the board should stop in place.

To carve, or turn, lean your upper body in the direction you want to turn. Let your body feel it: push your heels down, bend your knees into a deep crouch, use your arms. Soon you'll be able to work your way between slalom cones or any obstacle in your way. If you're heading downhill, carve from side to side, much like skiers carve their way down mountainsides to keep their momentum under control. Another way to turn is by resting your weight on the back leg and foot, lifting the front wheels lightly off the ground

Push tail down

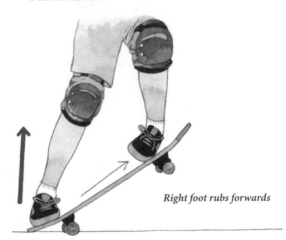

Back leg jumps up

Right foot rubs forwards

and moving the nose of the skateboard left or right before lowering the front wheels to the ground. You can practise this move on a carpet or on grass, stepping on the tail while pushing the nose in a 360° circle.

The Ollie is a basic skateboarding trick – all four wheels of the skateboard lift off the ground, with no hands holding the board. It looks like magic, but here's how to do it: start with your back foot on the tail and the front foot in the middle of the board. With your back foot, slam the board into the ground hard. Really believe in what you're doing and snap that board down. Then, do two movements pretty much at the same time: with your weight on your back foot, slide your front foot (which had been in the middle of the deck) towards the nose as – here comes the second movement – you jump your back leg into the air, where it will join your already-raised front leg. You'll need to really jump – get those feet up, propel your body into the air, lift your knees to your chest. The skateboard's nose is up, your whole body will rise, the tail will lift and for a brief and amazing moment you and the board will be suspended in midair. Get into a crouch position to absorb the impact of landing.

Yes, getting an Ollie takes practice. Daring girls know the two hundred times rule, that most things worth doing take patience and there's little we can't do after practising two hundred times. Skateboarding is like that too, although in the case of learning how to Ollie, it might take a thousand tries to feel the glory. But you will, and then you'll

Level out in the air

Land!

be ready to jump kerbs, work a ramp and, if you wish, enter the land of Wallies, kickflips, manuals and noseslides. You might even try a ripstick, which is a skateboard with two wheels, or just enjoy your newfound ability to travel further and faster than before on your own four wheels.

PLAYING CARDS:
HEARTS AND GIN RUMMY

---◆---

A Short History

EARLY PLAYING CARDS are believed to have originated in China, where paper was first invented, as a form of paper dominoes. The earliest references to playing cards in Europe featuring decks with four suits date from 1377. Cards back then were very expensive, as they were hand-painted, and they looked quite different from the design of cards today. The earliest cards from China had designs recognizable to players of Mah Jong: coins, or circles; and bamboo, or sticks. On their way from China to Europe, cards passed through the Islamic empire, where they gained cups, swords and court cards. Once in Europe, the generic court cards evolved into depictions of actual kings, knights and other royalty – hence the name 'face cards'.

The Italian, Spanish, German and Swiss cards did not include a queen – and in fact, even today, they still do not.

The basic familiar design of the cards – with hearts, diamonds, spades, and clubs, and court cards of Jacks, Queens and Kings – came from France, and with the invention of woodcuts in the fourteenth century, mass production became possible, making the French cards popular all across Europe.

There are hundreds of games that can be played with cards. Here are two popular and fun games for four or two people: Hearts and Gin Rummy.

HEARTS

Hearts is a trick-taking game for four players in which the object of the game is to avoid winning tricks (a set of cards) containing Hearts or the Queen of Spades. Hearts began its life in Spain around 1750 in a game called Reverse, the point of which was to lose tricks, not gain them. Eventually, about one hundred years later, Reverse fully morphed into the game we know today as Hearts.

'Tricks' are rounds of play in which each player puts a card face up on the table, and the player with the highest card wins all the cards – also called 'trick-taking'. But the real trick in this trick-taking game is that in Hearts players want to avoid winning tricks, because the lowest score wins.

Hearts uses a standard fifty-two-card deck. Aces are high, and there is no trump suit. To start, the dealer deals the cards clockwise so that all players have thirteen cards each. Each player then chooses three cards to pass: on the first hand, the cards are passed to the left; on the next hand, the cards are passed right; on the third hand, cards are passed across; and on the fourth hand, no cards are passed. Cards are passed stacked face down, and players must choose and pass their cards to the correct player before they can look at the cards passed to them.

The player who has the Two of Clubs goes first and must 'lead', or put down, that card. The play goes clockwise, with all the other players following suit (putting down a card of the same suit), if possible. That means each player must put down a Clubs card – if a player doesn't have any Clubs in this first hand, she can play any other card except for a Heart or the Queen of Spades. The player with the highest card takes the trick (stacking the cards face down next to her) and starts the next round. After the first trick, a Heart or the Queen of Spades can be used if a player doesn't have a card in the suit being led. Hearts can only be led (that is, be the first card in a trick) after a Heart has been 'broken' – played on a trick where a player couldn't follow suit.

Play continues until all the cards have been played. Then you add up the points for each player. Each Heart card gets one penalty point, and the Queen of Spades gets thirteen penalty points. The game is over when at least one person has one hundred points or more, and the winner is the player with the lowest score.

But there is one last 'trick' to be played in Hearts: a player can do something called 'Shooting the Moon'. That is when one player takes all the point cards (all Hearts and the Queen). The player who does this has her points reduced to zero, and everyone else automatically gets twenty-six points added to their score.

GIN RUMMY

This two-player card game is said to have been created by a man named Elwood T. Baker, who was inspired by an eighteenth-century game called Whisky Poker. Gin Rummy became popular in the 1930s, when Hollywood stars began playing the game in much the same way that celebrity poker is played today. Churchill even found time to play it.

To play the game, you need a standard fifty-two-card deck, and a pen and a pad of paper to keep score. You also need to know a bit of card talk to understand the game.

GIN VOCABULARY

Combination
Two cards of the same rank, such as Two-Two; or consecutive in the same suit, such as Two-Three of Clubs.

Count
The point value in a hand after deducting the total melded cards.

Deadwood
Cards that are not a part of any meld.

Gin
Ten melded cards.

Knock
To end the round.

Layoff
Getting rid of deadwood by incorporating it into the other player's melds, so that it is not counted.

Meld
Either a sequence or a set.

Sequences

A group of three or more cards of the same suit in consecutive order, such as Three-Four-Five of Spades, or Eight-Nine-Ten-Jack of Hearts.

Sets

A group of three or four cards of the same rank, such as Three-Three-Three or Jack-Jack-Jack-Jack.

TO PLAY

Decide who will be the dealer. The dealer then deals ten cards to each of the two players and places the remaining cards in a stack between the players. Another card is placed face up, next to the deck, to create a discard pile.

The goal of gin is to try to get your ten cards grouped in melds – sequences of cards (three or more cards of the same suit in order) or sets of cards (three or four cards of the same value). Before you take a turn, check to see if you have any melds, or any groups of cards that could easily turn into melds.

Each turn involves taking a card and discarding a card. The player who goes first draws a card from the deck. Now she must discard, choosing a card from her hand that is least likely to become part of a meld. High-point cards, like face cards, are good to discard if you can, since getting rid of them decreases your deadwood (the cards that are not part of any meld). Aces are low in this game: face cards are worth ten points each, Aces are one point and the other cards are equal to their numerical values (a Two card of any suit is worth two points, a Three card is three points, etc.).

When a player discards, the card must be placed face-up on the discard pile. The other player then has a turn, and she can draw from either the deck or the discard pile. Continue taking turns until a player 'knocks', or until only two cards remain in the deck (in which case the hand ends in a draw).

Knocking is when a player ends the round, and is signalled by a player literally making a knocking sound on the table. A player can only knock if she has ten points of deadwood or less. If you have zero points of deadwood, also known as 'going gin', you must knock. Otherwise, you don't have to knock unless you want to – even if you have ten points in deadwood or less, you can keep playing to try for gin or for a lower point count.

When you decide to knock, rap once on the table, lay down your cards face up, and add up your deadwood. The other player then lays down her hand and separates her deadwood from her melds. If she has any deadwood that can be incorporated into your melds, she can 'layoff' – that is, give them to you for your meld so they cannot be counted as her deadwood. After that, add up her total remaining deadwood. Subtract your deadwood from the other player's deadwood, and the answer you get is your score for this hand.

If you have zero points of deadwood, you must knock and call 'gin'. You get a twenty-five-point bonus for gin, on top of the points for the other player's deadwood (which she cannot layoff in this case).

If you knock and it turns out the other player has less deadwood than you, you get no points – but the other player scores not only the total of your deadwood minus hers, but twenty-five bonus points as well. That is called 'undercutting'.

After the cards have been counted and points totalled, gather up the cards, shuffle, and deal the next hand.

Keep playing until one of the players reaches one hundred points. Each player receives twenty-five points for each hand she won, and the player who reached one hundred points first gets an extra one-hundred-point bonus. The winner is the player with the most points after all the bonuses have been added.

HOW TO PADDLE A CANOE

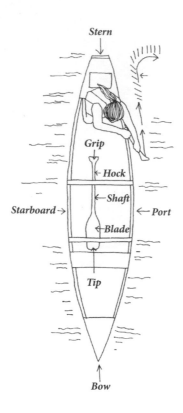

Stern

Grip

← Hock

←Shaft

Starboard→   ← Port

←Blade

Tip

Bow

THERE ARE LARGER, faster and more complex boats than a canoe, kayak or raft, but in none of those fancier boats can you feel the water so closely or slip into creeks and shallow wetlands to drift silently alongside cormorants, ospreys and swans.

Paddling a boat is an art that, like most pursuits, just needs practice to master. Huck Finn may have floated the Mississippi on a raft, and white-water kayaking is a thrill, but short of those, nothing beats a canoe for a water adventure.

Sometimes you need to be alone and your canoe is there for you. Other times you want to adventure with a friend and canoeing together is an exhilarating lesson in teamwork.

To learn to canoe, you should know these basic boat words, strokes and concepts.

The ordinary canoe stroke is the *forward stroke*. To paddle on the right, grab the grip (or top knob of the paddle) with your left hand and the shaft with your right. Put the paddle into the water, perpendicular to the boat, and pull it back and then out of the water. Keep your arms straight and twist your torso as you paddle. To paddle on the left, hold the grip with your right hand, the shaft with your left, and repeat.

To change course and return from whence you came, turn the boat and then paddle forward in the new direction. The *back stroke*, then, merely causes the boat to slow, or even stop. Put the paddle in the water slightly back, near the line of your hips and push towards the front, and then out.

It's important to remember that a canoe is not a bicycle. If you turn bicycle handlebars to the right, the bike will turn rightward. Not so in a canoe. When you paddle to the right, the boat will shift left. The opposite is true, too: left paddling pushes the boat to the right. Rotate your body as you paddle, since the power comes not from your arms exactly, but from your torso. With practice, you will learn to do this instinctively, using your hips and body weight to control the boat's direction.

Two-person canoeing is a delicate dance whereby the person at stern steers and gives directions while the person at bow paddles, changing sides at will to keep the boat in its line.

When you paddle alone it is essential to know the *J-stroke*, which, by means of a small flip at the end, keeps the boat in a straight line. The J-stroke is just that. As you paddle on the left side, draw the letter J (see the canoe illustration). On the right side, it will look like a mirror-image J, or a fishhook. In other words, put the paddle in the water close to the canoe and before your forward stroke ends, turn the paddle out and away from the boat; that's the J. Then lift the paddle out of the water and ready it to start again.

Some beginning canoers constantly move the paddle from right to left sides, but that's a quick way to tire your arms. Using a *C-stroke* to steer will allow you to paddle to one side more of the time. Start as with a forward stroke, but trace a C (on the left, or its mirror image on the right) in the water. When you do this, turn the blade so it's nearly parallel to the water.

This next stroke has many names, *crossback* being one of them. It's a stop. Drag the blade into the water and hold it still. Really, really hold the paddle tight against the water's rush. This stops the boat. It also turns it to that side, but this is not a suggested way to turn, since it slows the boat down too much.

One final stroke is perfect for when you find yourself in a cove with no company other than a family of mallards and two swans nestling on the nearby rock. The *quietest possible stroke* will break no water and make no sound. Put the paddle in the water and keep it there, making a figure eight, over and again.

Now, in the big scheme of life, all you need is a boat and a paddle. In real life, some additional gear is essential, the first being a lifejacket. It's itchy and annoying and you'll be tempted to leave it on shore. Don't. Please. It can save your life in bad weather. In a less dire circumstance, if you tip, it will give you a leg up as you grab your paddle and pull yourself into your boat.

Drinking water is necessary and, last but not least, bring a rope. Ropes are key to canoe adventures. You might find a stray canoe that needs to be towed to shore, or need to tie the canoe to a tree while you explore a riverbank. Perhaps the tide has gone out in a creek and you need to hop out of the boat and pull your canoe back to deeper waters. Lifejacket, water, rope and you're set.

Last tips: In general, the closer to the boat you paddle, the straighter it will go. To turn, paddle further from the boat.

Crouch low in the boat when getting in and out. Read the tide charts so you know where the water is.

Breathe deep, paddle smart and enjoy your voyage.

HOW TO PADDLE A CANOE

MARCO POLO AND
WATER POLO

———◆———

Access to a pool, lake, pond, creek, river, stream, ocean or garden hose is critical on a hot summer day. Contests are always fun: swimming stroke races (on your mark, get set, go!), diving and seeing who can make up the funniest jumps. Cannonballs are great fun, as you run off the diving board, hurl into the air, grab onto your legs and make a huge splash. Underwater tricks like handstands and multiple back flips are also a nice way to cool off, as are attempts to mimic the intricacies of synchronized swimming. On a rainy day, you

MARCO POLO AND WATER POLO

can watch old movies by water-ballet star Esther Williams for inspiration.

With water games, the main challenge is usually not the game itself, at least once you're on your way to mastering swimming – it's your nose, and how to keep water from rushing into it. You have three choices:

1. Breathe out sharply through your nose as you jump or duck underwater. The air coming out of your nose will keep water out.
2. Use one hand to hold your nose.
3. Find yourself an old-fashioned nose plug, the kind attached to the front of a rubber necklace. Clip your nose shut.

Thus prepared, below are a couple of aquatic games for those who can get to a pool or other slow-moving body of water.

MARCO POLO

The famed explorer Marco Polo was seventeen when he left Venice, Italy, to join his dad and uncle on a horseback journey to China. He did not return home for twenty-four years. While travelling, he befriended the Emperor Kublai Khan and was one of the first Western travellers of the Silk Road. He was fascinated by China's use of paper money and its intricate postal delivery system, innovations that far outstripped Europe's development at the time.

How Marco Polo's name got attached to the internationally known pool game, no one knows, but here are the rules.

You need at least three friends and everyone starts in the water. One person is It and her goal is to tag the other people. She closes her eyes, thus blinded (or you can use your handy bandana for a blindfold). Then she counts to five, or whatever number you all agree on. To try to find the other kids without seeing them, It must listen and sense where they are. Whenever she wants, she yells 'Marco'. Everyone in the game must immediately respond 'Polo'. The girl who is It uses the sounds of the other people's movements and voices to find and tag someone. Whoever she tags becomes the new It.

VARIATIONS

Now, there are some alterations you can employ to make Marco Polo more amusing and challenging. If you choose to, you can allow 'fish out of water'. This means the non-It players can get out of the pool. However, at any time, It can yell 'fish out of water' and if someone is out of the pool, that person automatically becomes the new It. If no one is out of the water, the other players often yell 'no'. (Hint: This can help It reorient and find them, too.)

You can also allow 'mermaid on the rocks', which is similar to 'fish out of water'. If someone is a mermaid on the rocks, she is sitting on the ledge of the pool or the lakeshore with only her feet in the water. Again, if It yells 'mermaid on the rocks', any mermaid becomes the new It. For either of these out-of-the-water variations, if It calls for fish or mermaids and there are none, she must do the start-of-game countdown again.

Another fun addition is 'alligator eyes', which allows It to call out 'alligator eyes' (or 'sub-marine', if you prefer) and then swim underwater with eyes open for one breath. Usually It is allowed to use this only once. We've heard of some places where It is allowed to go underwater and look around any time, but cannot move until she is above water with eyes closed or blindfold on again. We haven't played this one, but you may want to try it.

WATER POLO

While Marco Polo can thank the real Marco Polo for its name, water polo's comes from the game's rubber ball, which came from India, where the word for ball is pulu, hence polo.

Water polo was invented in England in the 1870s, though a similar kind of game may have been played in rivers in Africa and in flooded rice paddies in China many centuries before. While water polo claimed to resemble rugby, in practice it was more akin to underwater wrestling, with players hitting and ducking each other underwater with great regularity. Players would protect the ball by sticking it in their swimsuit and swimming underwater towards the goal. A much loved but extremely dangerous water polo feat had one player jumping off the backs of teammates and flying through the air, ball in hand, towards the opposing goal.

Good thing the more civilized 'Scottish' rules replaced the former free-for-all. The new rules instituted fouls for pushing and hitting, declared that the ball had to stay above water (no more bathing suit tricks!), and stated that only a player holding the ball could be tackled (thus lowering the number of players who ended the game in casualty).

HOW TO PLAY

A water polo team has six field swimmers and a goalie. Teammates pass the ball and keep it from the other side, until one of them can lob it into the goal and score. To move forward in water polo you swim with your head out of water, since you'll need to see where the ball is. To backstroke, you sit in the water, use your arms to make small short strokes and use the eggbeater kick to stay up and moving: as you sit in the water, bend your knees and circle each leg towards the other, like an eggbeater.

Rules

- ∗ You can touch the ball with your hands – though with only one hand at a time, which means you'll catch the ball and pass it quickly.

- ∗ Don't touch the bottom of the pool. This sport is about constant motion, no rest, and never touching the bottom.

- ∗ No pushing, pulling, hitting or holding on to the other players – that's a foul. Fouls are also called if you hold the ball underwater, touch it with two hands or hold on to it longer than thirty-five seconds; or if you touch the bottom, push off the side of the pool, or use bad language.

While Marco Polo will never be an Olympic sport, water polo is. Male Olympians have played water polo since 1900. Ever since the 2000 Olympics in Sydney, women's water polo has been on the roster, too and there's a terrific story behind its entry. After a decade or two of polite behind-the-scenes negotiation with the International Olympic Committee, the Australian women's national water polo team pushed the issue. The upcoming Olympics were on their turf, after all, and they wanted to compete. In 1998, members of the Olympic Committee were set to arrive at Sydney airport, in town for a planning visit. Led by their goalkeeper Liz Weekes – she's called the team's 'glamour girl' because she's also a model – the Aussie women water polo players put on their swimsuits and caps and strode through Sydney airport to meet them, and, very much in the public eye, they asked again to be included, and met with success.

Better yet, after fighting so hard to be included, the Australian women's team won the gold medal, with player Yvette Higgins scoring the winning goal during the last second of the championship game, to the applause of fans who filled the stadium.

DRAWING A FACE

— ◆ —

DRAWING IS SOMETHING you can do whether you're outside under a shady tree or inside listening to a summer rainstorm. All you need is paper, a pencil and rubber and your imagination.

1 Make an oval.

2 Draw a line down the centre of the oval from top to bottom. This guideline and the other lines you will be drawing in the next four steps should be dark enough to see but faint enough to be easily erased.

3 A little more than halfway down, draw a straight line across. (This will be where the eyes will go.)

4 Halfway between that line and the bottom of the oval, draw another line. (This will be where the nose ends.)

5 Draw another line halfway between the line you just drew and the bottom of the oval. (This will be where the mouth goes.)

6 Starting at the bottom of the oval and extending downward, draw two lines for the neck.

DRAWING A FACE

7 Using the lines you've made as guides, start sketching in the eyes, nose and mouth. Once you're happy with what you have, sketch in the hair.

8 To make sure your drawing is symmetrical, hold it up to a mirror. Crooked or lopsided areas tend to jump out at you when you look at your work 'backwards'.

9 When you've corrected any lopsidedness, and you're happy with the general look of the face you've drawn, you can start to rub out those guiding lines you made at the beginning and either continue to refine your work or bask in a job well done.

Tips for drawing anything

USE RELATIVE PROPORTIONS

Use your thumb or your pencil as a measuring stick to gauge the length and distance of what you're drawing. If you're drawing the tree in your backgarden, for instance, close one eye and hold up a thumb. When you hold your thumb next to the tree, is the trunk as long as your thumb? Twice as long? Is the treetop the same, or less, or more? Once you compare those measurements, you can apply them to your drawing to help create more accurate proportions.

USE A GRID

If you're working from a picture, instead of trying to attack the whole scene all at once, divide it into a grid of three-centimetre squares. You can do this by drawing a grid on a sheet of clear plastic (or, in a pinch, on clear plastic wrap) to lay over your reference material, or by cutting up a piece of paper into three-centimetre squares, laying them out over your picture or photo and removing one square at a time to reveal that three-centimetre square portion of the photo below. Divide the workspace of your sketchpad into a grid as well and transcribe what you see, one square at a time.

DRAW UPSIDE DOWN

Just like holding your artwork up to a mirror, drawing something upside down makes everything familiar look new and even a little strange. But that's a good thing, because it tricks your brain into breaking things down into basic shapes and patterns instead of automatically recognizing and categorizing what you see. When you think, 'I'm going to draw a nose', your brain is filled with everything it already knows about what noses look like — including what a 'bad drawing' of a nose looks like. And that may inhibit you from drawing to the best of your ability. When you look at a picture of a nose upside down and try to draw it, you're forced to rely on what you see — which certainly doesn't look like what your brain knows about noses. So you have to instead follow your instinct in replicating what you see. A rounded part here, a dark part here, a straight line there. Not a lot of opportunity for a chattery brain to jump in with a critique. Try this with a line drawing first: take a page from an old colouring book, place it upside down in front of you and try to draw what you see. (For a fun experiment, try drawing the same picture from the page right side up. Which one looks more like the original picture?)

KNOTS AND STITCHES

❖

A GOOD KNOT ENSURES that your boat will be there when you return, your tyre swing will hold, and your dog won't run into traffic. Here are a few useful knots with many everyday uses, and a few words on stitches, which come in handy for small repairs.

A piece of rope is all you need to begin. In each of our directions, 'rope' means the stable or standing part of the rope. 'End' refers to the part you are working with to make the knot, the working end. Make sure it's always long enough to do the job. 'Bight' is another word worth knowing; it's the part of the rope that becomes the knot.

1. STOPPERS

A stopper knot keeps a rope from slipping through a hole; it is the bulge at the end of a line. The most ordinary kind is called the overhand knot, or half knot. It's the knot you use to keep a thread in place when you start to sew.

Half knots are not very strong, but they are perfect for making the swing part of a rope swing. Tie four or five loose half knots near the bottom of the rope. Push them together, and tighten. They'll form a larger bulb that's perfect for sitting on as you swing. If you like, tie a half knot every few feet up the rope, for climbing or for holding on to while you do an arabesque (twisting the rope slightly around one ankle, and lifting your other leg gracefully behind you, like they do at the circus).

Safety note: For rope swings, you'll want to attach the swing to a tree branch using a stronger clove hitch or a tautline hitch. Make sure you tie the rope to a branch that extends far enough from the trunk so you can swing safely.

An alternative to the half knot is the Flemish knot, which you can also use any time you need a knot at the end of a line. It's both strong and lovely.

1. Make a loop at the top.
2. Cross the end behind and over to the left.
3. Wrap the end over and into the eye of the initial loop. You should see a figure eight.

4. Pull the end into the eye, or centre, of that loop.
5. Pull tight.

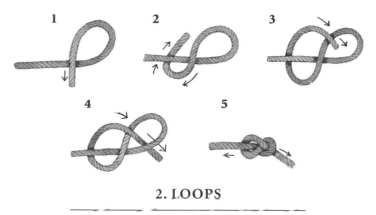

2. LOOPS

Once you've mastered the Flemish figure eight, you can make a loop the same way. Double up the rope or string. For hauling, tie the loop around your object, and lift or drag with the rope.

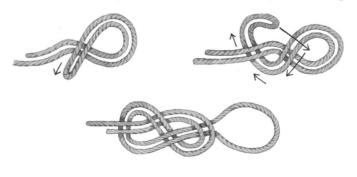

3. BENDS

Bends link two ropes together. When you need to repair a string that's broken, add new length to a rope or for any reason tie two ropes together, the square knot is what you want. Also called the Hercules knot, it was used by the Greeks and Romans as a healing charm. In *Natural History*, the Roman writer Pliny the Elder advised people to tie off their bandages with this knot, since it would heal the wound more quickly. Simple and reliable, this knot works best on string or thinner rope, and with any ropes of equal size.

Square knot
The classic formulation for a square knot is this: Left over right, right over left. Don't worry: in our experience, that's the kind of direction that makes more sense after you already know how to tie knots. So, try this: Loop A over loop B. Then wrap the ropes of B over the sides of, and into, loop A. Pull.

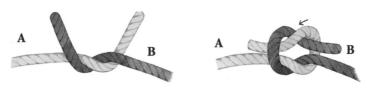

Square Knot

Sheetbend knot

If you're attaching the ends of a single rope, perhaps to tie off a friendship bracelet, try this: Make loop A. With loop B, thread the end into loop A, from the back. Then weave it out the bottom side, and under and across to the top of the loop. Next, bring rope A over the top side and through the loop, so it's next to the other side of rope B.

Sheetbend Knot

If you need something stronger, or your ropes are different sizes, use this variation, the sheetbend knot. The green one is the thicker rope.

4. HITCHES

Hitches tie an object or animal to a post, whether it's your dog at a friend's house, your horse to a tree in the shade, or your kayak to a pole on the dock while you go for a swim.

The tautline hitch is incredibly useful on camping and boating trips. Here's how to make it:

1. Start from the back and bring the end around the pole to the front

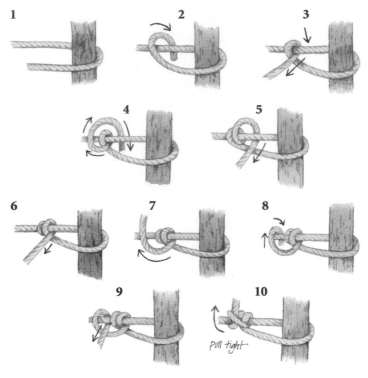

Tautline Hitch

KNOTS AND STITCHES

2. then over and behind the rope

3. and into the centre, or eye, and out the front.

4. Pull the end over and behind and into the centre once again

5 & 6. and pull out the front.

7. Take the end past the first two loops,

8 & 9. and wind it over and behind and into the centre

10. and pull tight.

The around-the-pole hitch moves around a pole. This is perfect for a dog who doesn't want to end up tangled, twisted, and stuck with a two-inch leash.

Loop the end one turn around the pole, front to back, and bring the end under and in front of the rope. Change course and lead it towards the top.

Wrap the end again around the pole, this time back to front, and then lead the end under and through the loop.

Finally, the timber hitch helps you drag a heavy object, like a log across a field. This knot is simple and also easy to untie, an important consideration in knots. It tightens in the direction you pull in, so make sure to use that to your advantage.

Around-the-Pole Hitch

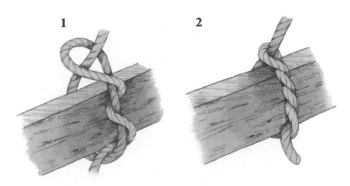

Timber Hitch

Wrap one turn, top to bottom, back to front. At the top, loop the end around the rope, to the left (this loop is important; the end must be wrapped around the rope it just came from). Tuck the end over, back, and around three or four times, and pull tight. The tucks must sit flat against the object for this knot to stay tight, since it is held in place by the rope's pressure against the object as you pull.

5. STITCHES

There will no doubt come a time when you need to mend your gloves, replace a button that's fallen off or sew the tear your trousers suffered while climbing rocks.

Cut your thread, push it through the needle, double the thread so it's extra strong, and place a knot – a gorgeous

Flemish stopper knot – at the end. You're ready. The stitches below can help you quickly mend any rip or tear that will inevitably occur in a daring life.

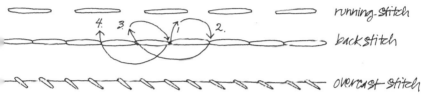

running stitch

backstitch

overcast stitch

MAKING YOUR OWN JEWELLERY

———◆———

MAKING YOUR OWN jewellery is great fun and not as difficult as you might think. The first thing is to pay a visit to a craft shop or a specialist bead shop to stock up on beads, catches and wire. Bead shops are great places to spend time rooting through bowls of pretty beads, imagining what you could make from them. Even better, prices start at only a few pence. If you don't live near a shop that sells beads, it's likely that someone you know has a basket full of odds and ends: buttons, fabrics, old beads – a treasure trove of things you can use again.

NECKLACES

Necklaces can be as simple or as complicated as you like. Whatever your design, you'll need a clasp, some wire and some beads. Simply thread the beads onto the wire, securing either end onto the clasp, and there you have it.

A slightly more complicated necklace, which will look really

impressive, is the floating bead necklace. You'll need several 'crimp' beads, which are beads that hold the main beads in place. Start in the middle of your necklace, feeding on one crimp bead and pressing it into place with some needle-nose pliers. It should be secure on the wire and not move. Then feed on your main bead – a single bead looks nice, or you can try several – and add another crimp bead afterwards, securing it into place again. Repeat as many times as you like to create a necklace where the beads look as though they are floating around your neck.

Once you've got the hang of the necklaces above, experiment. You can add more than one wire strand, layering several wires at different heights. Or try different sizes and feels of beads to create completely different looks.

BRACELETS

To make a bracelet, you can repeat the same steps as for the necklace, just on a smaller scale. Alternatively, try a bracelet on an elasticated cord simply by stringing beads onto a piece of elastic and securing with a knot.

EARRINGS

Earrings may seem a little more complicated but are worth the extra effort. You'll need two head pins (straight, non-bendable wire with a flat pin head on the bottom). String your beads onto the head pins, remembering to keep them the same on each pin: you wouldn't want uneven earrings! Then bend the top of the wire of the head pin into a hook using needle-nose pliers. Loop this onto an earring clasp, and you have a finished pair of earrings. This works for both pierced ears and non-pierced ears; just make sure you buy the right fittings.

SELLING YOUR WARES

You can turn your new-found skills into a way of making a bit of money, too. Why not set up a jewellery stall and sell your creations to friends, family and neighbours?

Calculating your profit

If you are setting up your jewellery stall to save up money for a Swiss Army knife or a special book, you must understand how to work out how much you earned – that is, your profit. Let's say you make two necklaces, five bracelets and a pair of earrings. From the sale of one of those necklaces, three bracelets and the pair of earrings you made £11.50.

First work out the profit, using this standard equation:

Revenue (money taken in) minus **Expenses** (materials) equals **Profit**

Revenue: You sold one necklace at £3, three bracelets at £2 each and a pair of earrings at £2.50, so you earned £11.50.

Expenses:	£
50 beads at 5p each	2.50
Wire	1.00
Clasps and fittings	0.75
Total expenses	4.25

Now plug the numbers into the equation: £11.50 – £4.25 = £7.25. You cleared £7.25 in profit.

THREE SILLY PRANKS

———◆———

Think boys are the only ones good at pranking? Think again! Here are three classic pranks for any daring girl.

STINK BOMBS

The old-fashioned kind, from the herb Valerian.

Head outdoors with the following:

* a small jar with a screw-on lid

* measuring spoons

* any kind of vinegar you can snag from the kitchen

* Valerian root powder – this is the key ingredient for a stink bomb. You can find this at any shop that stocks vitamins and herbal remedies. It comes in capsules that can be opened and emptied. If you can only find Valerian tea, mash it into a powder.

Mix one or more teaspoons of the powder with 2 teaspoons of vinegar, close the jar very, very quickly and shake. When you're ready to set off the stink bomb, open the jar (don't throw it), yell 'Skunk!' and run.

SHORT-SHEETING BEDS

For this prank you'll need to know the old-fashioned skill of making a bed, the fancy way, with tucked-in sheets.

Here's a refresher: Fit the bottom sheet over the mattress. Tuck the top sheet under the foot of the bed and along at least part of the sides. Lay the blanket on top, tuck that in too and then neatly fold the top edge of the sheet over the blanket, about fifteen centimetres or so. There. Stand back and observe your handiwork, because you will want the short-sheeted bed to look the same way.

To short-sheet a bed, you merely reposition the top sheet. Instead of tucking it in at the foot of the bed, tuck it in at the head of the bed. Lay out the sheet and halfway down the bed, stop and fold the sheet back towards the pillows. Place the blanket on top and fold a few centimetres of sheet on top for that neat, just-made look. This bed looks normal, but just try and stretch your legs out!

Important: Don't do this to anyone whose feelings will be hurt, only to those you know will laugh hard or at least giggle when they work it out.

FAKE BLOOD

Fool your friends with this easily prepared hoax.

You will need

* corn syrup

* cornstarch

* red food colouring from the pantry

* a jar with a tight lid

* a spoon

* an eyedropper

Red food colouring can stain, so wear old clothes, (although washing with very warm water and strong soap should clean it up). It is best to keep this prank outdoors.

Mix 4 small drops of food colouring, 2 teaspoons of water and 1 to 2 teaspoons of cornstarch in the jar, cover and shake. Pour in 2 tablespoons of corn syrup. Cover and shake again.

Use an eyedropper or a spoon to drip the fake blood where you want it. Make up a good story.

SHOOTING A BASKETBALL

———— ◆ ————

PUT YOUR ARMS out in front of you, elbows bent. Your stronger arm holds the ball, the weaker supports it. Your hands are close together, with the fingers spread. Flick your wrist back and push the ball into the air toward the net. Really push. For more fun, try a jump shot. Position yourself in classic ready position: two feet on the floor, legs slightly bent and shoulder-width apart, one foot slightly forward and shoulders squared to the basket. Hold the ball with your arms and hands high and cock your wrists back. Aim for the backboard. When you shoot, stay relaxed, look at the rim, uncock your wrists – and push the ball into the air while you jump up and slightly back. The power from your legs pushes through to your arms and sends the ball high into the air toward the net. You will be able to score many more points over the outstretched hands of defenders if you can perfect this fade-away jump shot.

HOW TO LOOK AT A LEAF

———— ◆ ————

EACH TREE HAS a unique and special leaf. Identifying an unfamiliar tree by its leaf means peering closely at its leaf, making note of distinctive features, consulting a good tree identification guide and narrowing down the options to find a match. With over half a million species of trees in the world and hundreds in the United Kingdom alone, you'll need to find a guidebook that is specific to your region. The following questions will speed you on the way to noticing details. Spread some leaves out before you and start navigating your way around the incredible world of trees.

Cypress

Oak

1 Is the leaf a needle like the Corsican Pine? Made of over-lapping scales like a Cypress? Or broad and flat like a Horse Chestnut?

2 If the leaf is a needle, are the needles single, like Norway Spruce, or clustered together, like the Corsican Pine? Do the needles lay flat, are they feathery or are they four-sided, so that the branch rolls between your fingers? Are the ends pointy or wide? Are there white lines underneath, a sure sign of a Juniper?

3 If the leaf is scaly, does it have a strong scent like a Cedar, or does it have vertical ridges like a Cypress?

4 If the leaf is broad and flat, is the arrangement simple, with one leaf attached to a stem, like the Oak, or is it

HOW TO LOOK AT A LEAF

compound, with several leaflets to a stem? On the compound leaf, are the leaves placed opposite each other, like an Ash, or are they alternate and asymmetrical?

Elm

5 Is the leaf's outline smooth and continuous, or toothy? Are the teeth small and close together, like the Elm, or coarse, like an Oak? Does each vein of the leaf end in a tooth? Are the teeth all the same size?

6 Does the leaf have lobes, like the Field Maple's lobes, and if so, how many and how far apart? Are the spaces between the lobes – called lobe notches – V-shaped or U-shaped, deep or shallow? Are there extra notches on each lobe?

Field Maple

7 Is the top of the leaf pointy, triangular, wavy or round? Is the base, where the leaf connects to the stem,

HOW TO LOOK AT A LEAF

Horse Chestnut

squared off and flat, round, heart-shaped like the Aspen, or V-wedged like the Oak? Are the sides of the top and base symmetrical, or do they vary? Is the stem long or short?

8 Do the leaf's veins radiate directly from the stem, like fingers, or are they connected to a main vein that runs through the leaf?

Soon you will be noticing even smaller details than we've thought of here.

As you collect leaves and match them to trees, you might want to create a leaf fieldbook. It might be a book of your neighbourhood's trees, or holiday-spot trees or merely a way to save leaves to identify later. Leaves can be pressed and preserved in several ways. You can stick them between two pages of a book and weigh the book down for several days.

Leaves can also be preserved in wax paper. Set the leaf between two pieces of wax paper and cover the pile with a thin towel. Turn the iron to medium hot, no steam, and iron over the towel to seal the wax paper around the leaf (ask an adult for help if you're not used to using a hot iron). The pages of wax-pressed leaves can be cut to a similar size and bound together for your book.

With leaves, there's always the chance to revisit your own early childhood: remember crayon rubbings of the undersides of leaves? Try updating that with new materials, like better paper, compressed charcoal and good quality artist's pencils. There's also that school science experiment, whereby the stem of a fallen leaf is placed into one half a cup of water mixed with ten drops of red food colouring (give the stem a fresh cut just before it hits the water) and everyone watches for three or four days until the veins and eventually the entire leaf turn red.

MAKING A SEINE NET

―――――◆―――――

A SEINE NET IS JUST a long fishing net used for dipping into the ocean to collect and study marine life.

What you need

* Seine netting. Ours is 2 metres deep and 5 metres long, with a half-centimetre mesh, but these measurements are flexible, depending on how big or small you want your net to be, and what's available. It's nice when the net has a bit of Styrofoam at the top edge to keep it afloat, and some metal weights on the bottom

to help it sink. Some seine netting comes this way. It can be bought at fishing shops.

* Two 2-metre poles or lengths of wood, to control the net, and to wind it up when you're finished.
* A large bucket, to keep your catch in water and to store the net.

Attach the shorter sides of the net to the poles. Do this by drilling a hole at each end of the pole (they might do this for you at a fishing shop, if you ask). Or, use a Swiss Army knife to whittle a channel at each end of the pole and wrap the rope there. Or forget the whittling and just wrap the rope very tight. If there's not already a thin rope at each corner of your net, find a small length of light rope or string and use that.

One person stands at the shoreline and holds a pole. The other person holds the second pole and wades into the water until the net is fully extended. Keep the top at water level and let the rest of the net sink. This is where the metal weights come in handy.

After a time, walk back to shore in a sweeping motion, keeping the net fully extended so that when you get to shore, you'll be a net-length away from your friend holding the other end of the net. As you get closer to shore, slowly change the net direction from vertical – where it is catching fish and other creatures – to horizontal, where you can scoop them up and lay out the net on the wet sand to see what you've got.

If you're not catching much of anything, change your position, or your location, or trawl a bit, walking around with the net stretched, giving more fish more time to end up in your hands. Both of you can walk further into the river or surf.

Throw back everything within a few minutes so that your catch can continue their lives at sea. Many towns have laws that tell you to throw the sea animals back where they belong, or else you will suffer a stiff penalty. (Some beaches ban large-scale commercial seine netting, but these small ones are usually okay.)

If you're going fishing, though, little minnows are good bait.

How to clean a shell

When your beachcombing and seine netting land you choice shells, here are two ways to clean them and turn them into long-lasting treasures.

1 Bury the shells 30 centimetres underground in your back garden and let the earthworms and all those soil bacteria do their work. This can take several months.

2 Boil for five minutes in a large pot, in a solution that is half water and half bleach. You'll see when the shells are clean. Take them out carefully with tongs, because the water will be scalding. Rinse with cool water.

HULA HOOPING

◆

THE REAL CRAZE FOR HULA HOOPING started in the 1950s in Britain, but the idea of spinning a hoop around your hips was not new. Children had been hooping with anything and everything from bamboo to grape vines to wood and metal for 3,000 years, all the way back to Egyptian times. But it wasn't until 1958 that the plastic hula hoop that we all know today was invented. A craze was born, and soon everyone was hooping!

DID YOU KNOW?

* The word 'hula' was added to 'hoop' after sailors visiting Hawaii in the eighteenth century noticed the similarity between hula dancing and hooping. The two have been linked ever since.

* The current world record for the longest hula hoop is held by Roxann Rose from America who managed to hoop for an amazing ninety hours in 1987. This was without a break, so no stopping to eat, drink or sleep.

* The greatest number of hoops used simultaneously to hula hoop is 100.

* The longest distance ever run while hula hooping is 100 metres.

* The largest hula hoop ever successfully hooped is a massive 15.3 metres.

* The strangest thing ever used as a hula hoop is a tractor tyre.

HOW TO HULA HOOP

It may seem obvious, but there is actually quite a skill to hula hooping. Here are some tips to get you started:

Stand with your legs about shoulder-width apart.

Start with the hoop against your back and spin it in whichever direction feels more comfortable. The trick now is not to try to rotate your hips with the hula hoop, but to move your hips up and down, shifting your weight from one foot to the other. It's trickier than it sounds but it will work! Then it's all about practice. Once you are comfortable with hooping around your waist, try to hoop around your wrist or your ankle. Or perhaps try adding another hoop for maximum effect.

CUSTOMIZING YOUR HULA HOOP

Hula hoops come in all different shapes and sizes, some even with flashing lights! But nothing is quite as satisfying as expressing your style and creativity and making a hoop your own. Here are just a few ideas; we're sure you'll come up with lots more.

* Try tying lengths of ribbon around the hoop at regular intervals. When you hoop, they'll spin out impressively.

* Grab some coloured sticky tape and wind it around the hoop, creating a spiral effect that will look even better once you're spinning.

* A slightly more fiddly option is wrapping your hoop in decorative paper, sticking it down with glue so it doesn't catch when you're hooping.

HULA HOOPING

MAKING YOUR OWN HULA HOOP

You can go one stage further and make your own hula hoop from scratch. This way you'll end up with a hoop exactly the right size for you.

* Start off with a length of tubing, around 2 centimetres in diameter. Hosepipe is good and can be found in most garden centres.

* Cut a length that, when in a hoop shape, comes to above your bellybutton.

* Using an inserted connector (available from DIY shops), push one end of the tube onto the connector. At this stage you can fill the tube with sand if you want to weigh it down. Then connect the other end of the tube to the connector, making sure it is securely fastened.

* Decorate to your taste, and then you are ready to impress your friends.

Happy hula hooping!

HIDEOUTS AND DENS

---◆---

EVERY GIRL SHOULD have a hideout or den of her own, and here are some ideas for making one. Several weekends may be spent sweating over the plans for a long-lasting outdoor Wendy house of wood beams and nails and real roofing tiles. But there are ways to make quicker work of this endeavour.

QUICK WENDY HOUSE

With 2-metre metal garden stakes, you can construct an outdoor Wendy house almost immediately. Garden stakes haven't the stability of wood beams, but the swiftness with which the walls go up easily makes up for that. Five stakes will do the trick.

The stakes come with footholds. Stand on them and they should push into the ground rather effortlessly. If there's a problem, a rubber mallet or a taller person can help; if it proves intractable, that may mean that there's a rock in the ground and you need to move the stake. Use one stake for each of the four corners. Set the fifth stake along one of the sides to create a space for the door.

Wrap the whole structure, except the doorway, with chicken wire or lighter-weight bird netting. Garden stakes have notches in them and you can attach the materials to the notches to form the basic wall. (Trim the bottom of the netting neatly at ground level, lest cats, birds or other small animals inadvertently get tangled inside; this happened to us.)

To add privacy, use large (disused) sheets or cloth as a second layer, or cardboard (you'll work out a way to attach these to the stakes). If you want a ceiling, the sheets or cloth will help, although they won't be waterproof, and rainwater will collect on top. You can use a tarpaulin, but the plastic can make the inside very hot. You'll work it out. A sixth stake, taller than the rest, can be added to the centre to create a sloped ceiling. From here, use string, rope, gaffer tape, wire, scissors, sticks, cardboard, plywood, and any other wood scraps you can find to build walls, create windows, ceilings and floors, and otherwise make it your own. There are no rules; it's your Wendy house.

LEAN-TO

A lean-to is a very primitive form of shelter that's little more than a wall or two and a roof. It's meant to keep you safe from the worst of the rain and wind, and often leans into existing walls or fences, hence the name. Find any tucked-in spot or corner, rig a tarpaulin roof with some ropes knotted to trees and lean a side of plywood against the house. Build up the front with branches, odd pieces of old fence your neighbours left out on bin day or even a picnic table turned on its side.

INDOOR HIDEOUT

The classic formula of sofa cushions, blankets, and the backs of settees and chairs is a good start for an indoor hideout, as is throwing blankets over the top of the dining room table (stacks of books on top help keep them in position).

You can improve upon these traditional dens. To make a hanging wall, screw a line of hooks or eyebolts into the ceiling. Run picture-hanging wire or clothesline rope through them. Attach clips or clothes pegs, and from these, dangle all sorts of sheets, light blankets, large swathes of cloth or oversized scarves to create a different kind of den.

JACKS

❖

JACKS, ALONG WITH MARBLES, is one of the oldest games in the world. Shop-bought jacks are six-pointed star-shaped objects, with a ball to bounce as we scoop them up, but in its early form the game was played with whatever was at hand – stones, small animal bones, or even crumpled-up paper.

Players decide who goes first by 'flipping' or using any rhyming game to determine the first player. Flipping means tossing jacks in the air and trying to catch as many as you can on the back of your hand. The player who catches the most gets to go first.

To begin play, toss the ten jacks onto the playing surface. Then bounce the ball in the air, pick up one jack using your throwing hand and catch the ball in the hand holding the jack before the ball bounces. (Place the jack you've collected in your other hand or off to the side before you try to pick up another one.) Do this again, picking up one jack at a time without the ball bouncing twice, until you've picked up all ten jacks. This is 'onesies'. Once you've done that successfully, move on to 'twosies': scatter the ten jacks again and this time pick up two jacks at a time. Do this until you've picked up all ten jacks. Continue to 'threesies', where you pick up the jacks three at a time, 'foursies', four at a time, and on all the way to 'tensies'.

(When there are 'leftovers' – one jack in 'threesies', two jacks in 'foursies' – you pick them up individually. If you pick them up before you've picked up the groups, that is known as 'putting the cart before the horse', and you must call 'cart' as you pick up the individual 'leftover' jacks. 'Threesies' has three groups of three and one jack in the 'cart'; 'foursies' has two groups of four and two jacks in the 'cart', etc.)

Your turn is over when you don't pick up the correct number of jacks, you miss the ball or the ball bounces. When it's your turn again, start up where you left off – if you lost your turn on 'twosies', start at 'twosies'. The winner is the player who is able to pick up the largest number of jacks successfully.

TIPS AND VARIATIONS

Usually, only one hand may be used to throw the ball and pick up the jacks, but play can be simplified to allow two hands. You can also make it more difficult by only allowing players to use their 'bad' hands (right hand for left-handed players, left hand for right-handed players).

OTHER JACKS LINGO

Kissies
When two jacks are touching. They can be separated by calling 'Kissies!' while a player moves them apart.

Fancies
Complicated ways of picking up the jacks, like not being allowed to touch the jacks you don't pick up.

Around the World
Toss the ball, circle the ball with your hand and then pick up jacks before the ball bounces.

Cats in the Well
Make a loose fist with the thumb and first finger of your non-throwing hand. The jacks you pick up ('cats') are dropped through the opening (the 'well').

Eggs in the Basket, or Picking Cherries
Toss the ball, pick up the jacks and transfer the jacks to your other hand before catching the ball.

Pigs in the Pen
Make an arch with the thumb and first finger of your non-throwing hand. Then toss the ball, flick a jack through the arch and then catch the ball.

Pigs over the Fence
Make a 'fence' with your non-throwing hand by putting your hand on its side, thumb facing up. Toss the ball, transfer the jacks to the other side of your 'fence' and catch the ball.

Picking who's it

Rhymes to determine who goes first can be used for any game, from jacks to tag to board games to truth or dare. Here are some fun schoolyard ways of figuring out who gets to be first.

Eeny, Meeny, Miny, Moe
(Point at each player for each word said; whoever the rhyme ends on is out and you start again until there is only one person left who is 'it'. That person gets to go first.)

> *Eeny, meeny, miny, moe*
> *Catch a tiger by the toe*
> *If he squeals let him go,*
> *Eeny, meeny, miny, moe.*
> *O. U. T. spells out*
> *And out you must go.*

One Potato
(Players put their fists in a circle. The 'potato peeler' puts her fist on the players' fists as she says the words. Whoever lands on 'more' removes her fist. The last player left goes first.)

> *One potato, two potato*
> *One potato, two potato, three potato, four.*
> *Five potato, six potato, seven potato, more.*

PLAYING HOPSCOTCH

———— ◆ ————

BELIEVE IT OR NOT, hopscotch got its start not as a playground game, but as a military exercise. During the early Roman Empire in ancient Britain, Roman soldiers ran through 30-metre-long rectangular courses wearing full armour to help improve their footwork. Roman children drew up their own version of these courses, shortening the length and adding a scoring system, and the game of hopscotch was born.

The word *hopscotch* comes from *hop*, of course, meaning to jump, and *escocher,* an Old French word that means 'to cut'. The game as we know it dates back to at least 1801, and now hopscotch is played all over the world. In France, the game is called *Marelle*. Germans play *Templehupfen,* and kids in the Netherlands play *Hinkelbaan*. In Malaysia hopscotch is called *Ting-ting* or *Ketengteng,* and in India it's called *Ekaria Dukaria*. In Vietnam it's known as *Pico,* in Chile it's *Luche,* and in Argentina and many Spanish-speaking countries, it's called *Rayuela*.

COURTS

Make your own court using chalk on a pavement or driveway, or by using masking tape on a floor or carpet indoors.

Traditional courts look something like this:

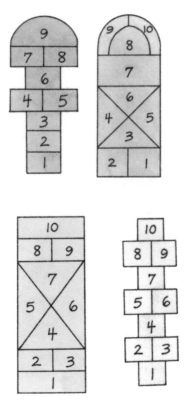

Super-old-fashioned courts had six boxes in a stack from one to six or three sets of two boxes:

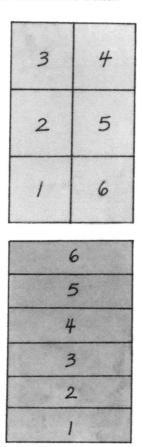

Fancier versions include the Monte Carlo and the Italian:

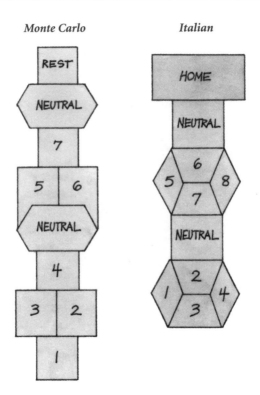

Monte Carlo *Italian*

Or, you can always make up your own style of hopscotch court!

RULES

Nearly every girl knows the basic rules for hopscotch, but there are some interesting variations to liven things up.

In the most basic game, the first player stands behind the starting line to toss a marker (a rock, a penny, a beanbag, a button) in the first square. The marker must land in the correct square without bouncing out or touching a line. The player should hop over the first square to the second on one foot, then continue hopping all the way to the end of the court. Side-by-side squares can be straddled, with each foot on a square, but single squares must be hopped on with just one foot. A square with a marker in it must be hopped over, and any neutral, or safe, squares may be jumped through in any manner a player wishes.

When a player gets to the end of the court, she turns around and hops back through to the beginning, stopping to pick up her marker on the way. If she makes it to the end without jumping on a line or putting two feet down in a square, she can continue her turn by throwing the marker into square number two and trying again. If a player steps on a line, misses a square, falls, or puts two feet down, her turn is over. When it's her turn again, she starts where she left off. The winner is the first player to complete one course of hopping up and back for every numbered square.

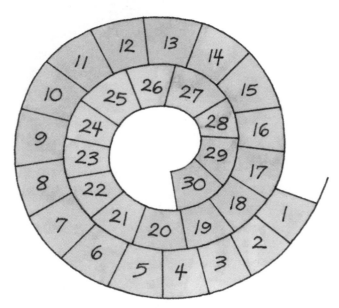

Escargot *(snail) or* **La Marelle Ronde**
(round hopscotch)

VARIATIONS

A French version of hopscotch is played on a spiral court and called, because of its shape, *Escargot* (snail) or *La Marelle Ronde* (round hopscotch). The court is drawn as a big snail or shell-like spiral and then sectioned into squares, the number of which is limited only by the size of the spiral itself. In this version, each player hops on one foot to the centre of the spiral and back out again. When a player is able to complete the full circuit, she can mark one square with her initials, and from then on she is allowed to have two feet in that square. The other players must hop over it. The game is over when all squares are marked (or if no one can reach the centre), and the girl who wins is the one who has her initials in the most squares.

This variation, allowing the player to initial a square, can also be adapted for the traditional version of the game. After a player has completed one hopscotch sequence successfully, jumping all the way up and all the way back, she can throw her marker onto the court, and wherever the marker lands she can place her initials. Then that square is hers, and she is allowed to have two feet in it when hopping, while the other players must hop over it. In this version, each player is only allowed to initial one square per game.

Another variation, which can be used with traditional straight courts as well as with spiral courts, involves the player holding her marker between her feet and hopping from square to square on two feet without letting go of the marker or stepping on the lines.

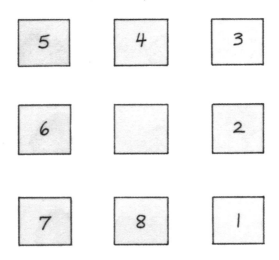

Toss-and-Reach Hopscotch

In Toss-and-Reach Hopscotch, a player throws her marker into the centre square, then hops to each square in order. From each square, she must reach in to pick up her marker without losing her balance or stepping on any lines.

In Agility Hopscotch, the player must hop back and forth across the centre line without touching any lines or losing

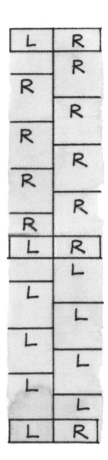

her balance. She must hop on her left foot in squares marked L and on her right foot in squares marked R. She may rest with both feet down where the L and R are marked opposite each other.

Agility Hopscotch

TRACKING ANIMALS

———— ◆ ————

THE WORLD IS teeming with animals. Whether in the city or suburbs, your backgarden or nearby woods, animals are everywhere and you can find them – you just need to know where to look. Try the intersections of terrains: between a wooded area and a stream or between a field and a stream. Animals need food, many need water and they need cover, so look for thick spots of trees and brush or any place that an animal can hide from a predator, as well as trails and clearings they might use to get from shelter to food and back again.

HOW TO FIND AN ANIMAL

Option one: wait. Find a perch in a tree or on the ground. Animals will run when they sense movement and repeated movement especially, so sit (or stand) and wait very, very silently for as long as it takes for an animal to come near. You might have a personal secret spot that you visit regularly or a new place each time you go looking for deer, rabbits or voles. In either case, breathe quietly and stay still. Let your ears hear as much as they can. Practise a wide angle of vision, where you scan left to right and right to left from the corners of your eyes without moving your head.

Option two: search for clues everywhere, from a bullfrog's loud croak to the delicate toe-print of a ringed plover in the sand. The most noticeable clues are the tracks made by an animal's heel pad, claws and inner and outer toes. Scan the ground for footprints or for any indentations. Depending on how wet or dry the ground is, you may barely see the full footprint that shows up so well in light mud, snow or sand.

Tracking guidebooks show pictures of each animal's front and hind prints and they measure the print's size and illustrate the track's patterns when the animal is walking slowly or bounding along. When you find a track, study it closely, measure, look for the next one to learn where the animal was headed and, based on how far apart the tracks are, how fast they were trying to get there. If you are miles from the nearest animal track guide, remember or sketch the track the best you can and identify it later.

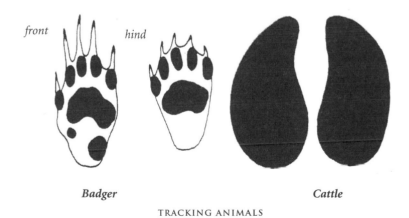

front   *hind*

Badger   **Cattle**

TRACKING ANIMALS

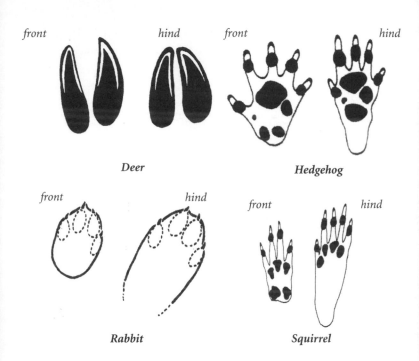

front   *hind*   *front*   *hind*

Deer   **Hedgehog**

front   *hind*   *front*   *hind*

Rabbit   **Squirrel**

Admittedly, animal tracks can be hard to find. Unless it's been raining or there's been snowmelt or you're down by a creek, many footprints don't hold for long on forest floors, covered as they are with evergreen needles or decaying oak leaves. In such cases, seek out other signs of animal life. Listen for sounds of animals moving. Notice any bent grass, broken twigs or tree scuffs and scratchings made by claws.

These are signs that animals have been nearby, as are leaf bites and chews, or browse lines, where deer have eaten the leaves of a tree up to their standing height. Other intriguing animal signs are empty spots in otherwise vegetation-crowded places, packed-down trails and corridors where animals have travelled, small openings into larger brush or bushes and small trees that have been crushed, squashed or otherwise moved out of place. Follow all signs and think like

an animal wanting food and shelter and you never know what you'll find.

WHEN YOU FIND AN ANIMAL

At last a deer or rabbit has come your way. What do you do? Freeze like there's no tomorrow. Those ears on the sides of an animal's head are made for picking up the slightest movement and sound and when they hear you, they'll run.

The stalk walk is the best way to move closer or to follow. Each time you lower a foot to the ground, land on the outside of the ball of your foot. Very lightly and very slowly roll onto the entire ball of your foot, feeling the ground beneath and then decide whether to stay on the ball of your foot or let the whole foot touch the ground. Then and only then, in no hurry at all, slink your body weight forwards to your front foot. The slower you walk, the quieter you can be, because leaves and twigs underfoot won't snap, they'll silently bend and mash. Try a super slow walk, where one step takes sixty seconds. (By the way, the stalk walk is great for any kind of spy activity.) You can bend your knees into a crouch to keep low and even slide your arms to the ground for a stalking crawl (always landing on the outside of your knees and hands and rolling in) and eventually working all the way down to the quietest belly crawl ever.

If no bears are out...

If you've had no luck finding any nonhuman animals, you can always play 'Track the Bear' with your friends and practise your tracking skills. One person is the bear, deer or any animal you choose. She runs ahead with a several-minute head start and follows whatever path she chooses, for as long as she wants. Every few steps, the 'bear' drops some beans (or some other non-polluting food). The trackers follow and collect the trail of beans till they find the 'bear'.

MAKING AND FLYING A KITE

❖

AS MARY POPPINS SO RIGHTLY SAYS, flying a kite is one of life's pleasures. And flying a kite you have made yourself is the best way to do it. Here's how:

Take two sticks of wood – the sort of bamboo used to prop up plants works well – one longer than the other. Form a cross with the two sticks and tie securely at the middle so that they are at right angles to each other with the shorter stick being horizontal.

Cut a notch into both ends of the sticks and wind some string around them to form a rectangular frame of string secured in the notches of the sticks. This is your frame.

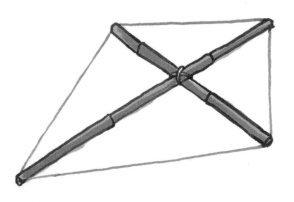 

Cut your paper sail so it is the same shape as the frame but about 10 centimetres larger on all sides. Use thick, strong paper for this. Lay the sail on a table, with the frame on top of it, centred so there is the same amount of paper on each of the sides. Fold the paper over the string and tape down securely.

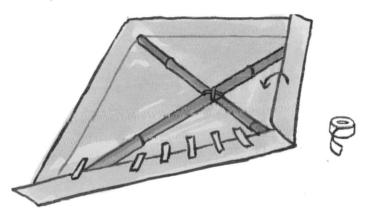

Tie a piece of string to the bottom of the upright stick, and one to the top. These two strings should be long – as long as you can make them – as they will be the string with which you fly the kite.

The final touch is to make a tail for your kite. Tie a long piece of string to the bottom of the upright stick and tie ribbons around that string at regular intervals as decoration.

Now wait for the next windy day so you can show off your kite!

MAKING AND FLYING A KITE

Let's Go Fly a Kite

With tuppence for paper and strings
You can have your own set of wings
With your feet on the ground
You're a bird in flight
With your fist holding tight
To the string of your kite

Oh, oh, oh!
Let's go fly a kite
Up to the highest height!
Let's go fly a kite and send it soaring
Up through the atmosphere
Up where the air is clear
Oh, let's go fly a kite!

When you send it flying up there
All at once you're lighter than air
You can dance on the breeze
Over houses and trees
With your fist holding tight
To the string of your kite

Oh, oh, oh!
Let's go fly a kite
Up to the highest height!
Let's go fly a kite and send it soaring
Up through the atmosphere
Up where the air is clear
Let's go fly a kite!

MAKING AND FLYING A KITE

MAKING AND FLYING A KITE

SWINGBALL

———◆———

SWINGBALL REQUIRES a fast mind and equally fast hands to send the ball spiralling around the pole for a win. This was our favourite game growing up and we'd love to see more swingball courts – and maybe some day swingball as an Olympic event.

At its most basic, swingball involves a ball – similar to a volleyball but somewhat squishier – tied to the top of a 3 metre pole by a rope. Two players try to hit the ball in one direction so that the rope winds completely around the pole. (But swingball is also fun to play by yourself – in your garden when no one's around. You can practise and make up games for yourself, too. Like trying to duck before the ball hits you in the head.) Actual swingball courts have a circle drawn on the ground around the pole and are divided in half. A drawn circle isn't necessary, but you should expect to need about 2 metres of space all around the pole and each player should stay on her own side of the circle.

RULES

The rules of swingball are deceptively simple: two people stand opposite each other, one person serves by hitting the ball in one direction around the pole and the other tries to hit the ball in the opposite direction around the pole. The first

SWINGBALL

player to get the rope wrapped completely around the pole is the winner.

Because the server has a big advantage (she gets to hit the ball first), players can decide to play matches instead of single games. The total number of games comprising the entire match is up to the players to decide, but the winner must win by at least two games. Another way to decrease the serving advantage is to have the player who doesn't serve choose which side of the circle she is on and which direction she is hitting.

FOULS AND VIOLATIONS

How seriously you take fouls is something that needs to be decided before the game. Fouls include:

* Stepping across the centre line.

* Server hitting the ball twice at the beginning before the opponent hits it once.

* Hitting the ball twice while it is still on your side of the circle.

* Reaching around the pole and hitting the ball.

* Catching or holding the ball.

* Throwing the ball.

* Touching the pole with any part of your body.

* Hitting the rope with any part of your body.

If you only have a few players, you can treat these fouls as mere violations and resume the game by stopping the ball and returning it to where it was wrapped when the violation occurred. The non-violating player gets to serve, and then either player can hit the ball. If a player racks up three violations, the opponent automatically wins.

If the two players commit a violation at the same time, they must do a pole drop to start the game again. Both players hold the ball with one hand, lifting it about three feet away from the pole, directly over the line dividing their two halves of the circle and then let go of the ball at the same time. The ball should hit the pole and then either player can hit it to continue the game.

No matter how you decide to play, the only absolute game-ender is grabbing the pole. If a player does that, she immediately loses the game.

EQUIPMENT

The Ball
A swingball is the only piece of equipment that you must purchase specifically for the game and is similar to a tennis ball. It will have either a loop sticking out of the surface or a recessed spot on the surface of the ball to attach the rope.

The Pole
The best pole for the job is a steel pipe 3 metres long and 5 centimetres in diameter sunk 30 centimetres into the ground, with an eyebolt run through the pole about 10 centimetres from the top for attaching the rope. This may be a good time to take a field trip to your local DIY shop. But with a good eye you might be able to spot a likely pole around town that will serve nicely for the game. Just remember to untie the ball and take it home with you when you are finished.

MAKING A SWINGBALL COURT IN YOUR GARDEN

Here's your shopping list:

* Steel pipe, 3 metres long, 5 centimetres in diameter

* Steel pipe, 50 centimetres long, slightly wider than 5 centimetres in diameter

* Eyebolt with nut (for attaching the rope to the top of the pole)

* Drill and bit capable of drilling through metal

* Concrete mix

* Swingball

* Rope (if not included with the swingball)

MAKING THE COURT

Drill a hole through the pole about 10 centimetres from the top for the eyebolt, and put the eyebolt in place.

Dig a hole in your lawn, gravel driveway or garden about 70 centimetres deep, with a 50-centimetre diameter.

Pour in 15 centimetres of concrete and let it set.

Stand the 50-centimetre-long pipe in the hole and add concrete around the pipe to fill the hole (it's a good idea to have something to keep the pipe in place while the surrounding concrete sets; also, the pipe should protrude just above ground level, but not so much that it sticks up enough to get nicked by a lawn mower).

Once the concrete is set, slide the pole into your concrete-and-pole base (this should be a solid, tight fit, but the long pole is removable).

Attach the rope and ball.

WATERCOLOUR PAINTING
ON THE GO

❖

ONE OF THE MOST ENJOYABLE ways to begin water-colour painting is to work outdoors, when the weather is nice and the light is good. Working outdoors is also great because nature is a fabulous subject for beginners to paint. Unlike trying to paint, say, a family portrait, or a picture of your friend, a landscape is a forgiving subject: even if you aren't able to capture the rolling hills and colourful flowers perfectly, your painting can still resemble an outdoors scene. (And you can always call it 'impressionistic' if it doesn't!) Here is what you'll need in your travelling watercolour kit.

* **Brushes**
  Bring an assortment of round and flat watercolour brushes in a variety of sizes (0, 2, 4, 8, 12). Synthetic sable is an economical, long-lasting alternative to the more expensive pure sable bristles.

* **Brush holder**
  A flat bamboo mat that can be rolled up and tied with a ribbon or string. Weave a piece of white elastic band through the lower third of the mat and insert brushes. Roll up and tie!

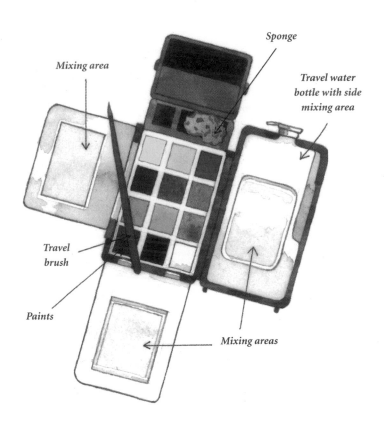

Sponge

Mixing area

Travel water
bottle with side
mixing area

Travel
brush

Paints

Mixing areas

Round
No.12

Round
No.4

½"
flat

Round
No.8

Round
No.2

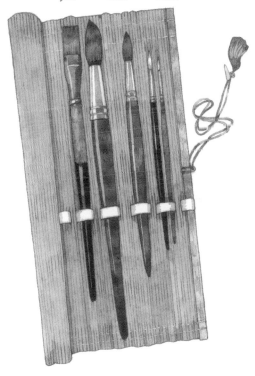

* **Travel-sized palette**
  Make sure the mixing area is large enough and that there's a good range of colours (red, orange, yellow, green, blue, violet, yellow ochre, burnt sienna).

* **Water containers**
  Two plastic collapsible water containers (they look like Chinese lanterns), or plastic jars – one for clean water and one for dirty.

* **Bottled water**
  If you're not near a water fountain or a bathroom with a sink, bring your own bottled water.

* **Paper, or a watercolour block, A3**

* **A sharp tool to remove sheets of paper from the block**

* **A No. 2 pencil and a kneaded rubber**

* **A towel to sit on, or a small beach chair**

Never leave your watercolour brush standing in water – it will ruin the bristles. Instead, keep the brushes on your bamboo mat. Let them dry in the air.

Clean your brushes before adding a new colour (especially when changing from dark to light hues).

If you wish to work on a separate sheet of paper rather than a block, use watercolour masking tape to secure all sides and edges of the paper to a board. Not doing so will allow air to get underneath and buckle the paper.

Do not overwork your painting! Wait for an area to dry completely before adding more water or pigment. Too much water can break down the fibres in the paper and make it look too 'scrubbed'. As with so many things in life, less is more.

Less water will give you a more opaque, darker colour. More water will yield a more transparent, lighter colour.

Lightly sketch your landscape or seascape in pencil before starting – you can always erase pencil marks, once the paper is completely dry, with a kneaded eraser. Darker, heavier lines are more difficult to remove.

GREAT WATERCOLOUR ARTISTS TO CHECK OUT

Beatrix Potter (nineteenth-century British watercolourist)

Sara Midda (contemporary British watercolourist and designer)

John Singer Sargent (American, nineteenth – early twentieth century)

Charles Demuth (American, early twentieth century)

Carl Larsson (Swedish illustrator, late nineteenth – early twentieth century)

Charles Reid (contemporary American watercolourist)

JMW Turner (British, nineteenth century)

Albrecht Dürer (German, Northern Renaissance)

Phansakdi Chakkaphak (contemporary Thai botanical watercolourist)

Charles Rennie Mackintosh (Scottish, late nineteenth century)

GARDENS, ALLOTMENTS AND WINDOW BOXES

---◆---

GROWING YOUR OWN fruit and vegetables is a lot of fun and very satisfying. You don't need a lot of space – you can even grow things in window boxes if you don't have access to a garden. What you do need is a little time, a little effort, some sunshine, some rain and a lot of patience.

ALLOTMENTS AND VEGETABLE GARDENS

These can be as large or small as the space you have available. Make sure you ask before digging up someone's prized lawn,

though! Mark out the area with pegs and string and start by preparing the ground. You'll need to cut down any tall plants and brambles and dig out all the weeds too. Then turn over the soil with a spade, loosening it and making it easier to work with.

Now your area is prepared, the most important thing you can do is get your plans in order. The more organized you are, the better your produce will be. First of all, work out which way is north so you can plant your seeds in the spots that work best for them. Then note which areas get a lot of sun and which are more shady.

Now all you need to decide is which vegetables you like! There's no point in growing vegetables that will go uneaten because in a good year your harvest is likely to be plentiful. Growing from seed is the most satisfying way to go, and you'll need to follow the instructions on the packets about when to sow and when to harvest as each vegetable varies. Some will need growing indoors first and then transplanting outside.

Once you have sown your seeds, make sure you tend your garden carefully, removing weeds and pests regularly, and keeping the plants watered. Friends are always happy to help out if you go away. Make sure you label your seeds clearly using a waterproof pen so you know what you have planted and where!

A SHORT HISTORY OF ALLOTMENTS

Growing your own vegetables has long been popular, but allotments have their own history born more of necessity than you might realize. Allotments are usually found in built-up areas and are large plots of land divided into

smaller sections that are allotted (therein the reason for the name) to individuals. Allotments have been popular since the eighteenth and nineteenth centuries when most towns were surrounded by land set aside for allotments. The popularity of allotments increased as part of a campaign by Britain's wartime government in the 1940s. At the time Britain imported a large proportion of its food, but the seas around our islands were full of enemy ships and it was impossible to bring in enough food for everyone. So the government encouraged people to 'Dig for Victory' by producing their own food. If the people could feed themselves, they would be strong enough to defend their borders and defeat the enemy! It was seen as your patriotic duty to grow your own fruit and vegetables but it was also much more productive than queuing at the local shops for the sparse supplies that were available to buy with ration coupons.

After the end of the war, as rationing drew to an end, it was housing that Britain needed most urgently, so many allotments were covered over by new housing to replace the old that had been destroyed by German bombs.

Today allotments are still available, but as there are fewer of them there can sometimes be a waiting list. Allotments are run by local councils, so get in touch with your council who can tell you how to go about getting an allotment in your area.

WINDOW BOXES

If you don't have access to a garden or allotment, don't worry: there is plenty that you can grow in a simple window box.

First make sure that your window box is securely fastened – you don't want it becoming loose and falling off the sill. A chain and two hooks fastened to the wall should do the trick.

Your box needs to be well drained, so fill the bottom with bits of broken crockery.

There are certain plants that will work better in window boxes than others, so stick to these. Here are a few ideas to get you started:

* Herbs: Mint, rosemary, chives, thyme, basil, oregano and sage all work well in window boxes.
* Cherry tomatoes.
* Lettuces: Rocket, lamb's lettuce and bijou all work well. Try sowing in sections so you can harvest one section as the others are growing.
* Radishes: Very easy and quick to grow.

GROW BAGS

If you have a small amount of outside space but no earth, grow bags are a great way of growing things. Cucumbers, sweet peppers, courgettes and aubergines all grow well in grow bags. Make sure you keep them well watered, though.

Whatever the size or shape of your plot, you should be able to grow some delicious fruit and vegetables. And remember, food you grow yourself always tastes better than any you can buy from the shops.

Fruit and Vegetables You Can Grow			
What to Grow	**When to Plant**	**When to Harvest**	**Top Tips**
Potatoes	March	June–September	Start with a seed potato and allow it to sprout tubers. Start this in January/February by standing your potatoes on a windowsill, out of direct sunlight. Then plant outside in March.
Courgettes	March–May	August	You need to propagate the seeds indoors and then transfer to your outdoor plot in May. Courgettes provide beautiful yellow flowers that are also edible.
Tomatoes	January–May	July–September	There are lots of varieties of tomatoes, including cherry tomatoes, which can be grown in hanging baskets. They all need to be propagated indoors to start with.

Salads	April–September	April–September	Salads are very easy and quick to grow, so you can keep resowing and regrowing them around every four weeks. Plant them right into the ground, or alternatively you can grow them in window boxes.
Rhubarb	October–December	May–June	It is best to grow rhubarb from young plants rather than from seed. Make sure you don't eat the leaves, though, as they are poisonous!
Strawberries	June–September	June–September	Again it is better to start with young plants than to grow from seed. Plant outside in June and check the plants every day for signs of slugs as these can destroy your strawberries.

TREE SWING

What you need

* Wood, 60 centimetres × 20 centimetres long
* Rope
* Two eyebolts, 20 centimetres long, with a 1-centimetre thread, two nuts and four washers
* A tennis ball, a sock, and some string
* Drill with 1-centimetre bit

THE HARDEST PART of building a tree swing is finding a well-suited branch. We can tell you that a tree-swing branch should be at least 20 centimetres in diameter, but on a tree tall enough for a swing, that can be difficult to measure precisely. You'll also need a strong rope long enough to get around the branch and down to the ground and back up again.

Your swing should not be on a birch tree, because those rubbery branches readily bend. Look for a hardy oak or maple. The spot on the branch where you hang your swing should be far enough from the trunk so no one is hurt when they swing, but close enough so the branch is still strong.

The second hardest part is getting the rope up and over the branch. To forestall several hours of standing with a rope and squinting into the sun, we have a strategy to suggest:

* Put a tennis ball in an old sock. Wrap string around the sock and make a knot so the tennis ball stays put, and make sure you have enough string on the skein so it can unfurl the length up to the tree branch, and back down again.

* Stand under the tree and aim the tennis ball in the sock over the branch. It may take a few tries, but it is much easier than just flinging the rope up to the branch.

* Once up and over, the tennis-ball sock will land near your feet, trailed by a long strand of string. Knot the string to the rope to be used in the tree swing. (Try a sheetbend knot, it's designed to join different sized ropes.) Pull the string until the rope is over the branch. You might want to toss the ball/rope combo over again, to double-loop the rope over the branch. When all is in place, detach the string. The rope is set.

The easiest part is making the seat and procuring a long length of knot. Find or cut a 60-centimetre-long piece of 20 centimetre-wide wood. Draw a line down the centre, lengthwise, and measure 5 centimetres in from either side.

That's where to drill the two holes. Put an eyebolt through each hole, with a washer above the wood and a washer and nut below it. Knot the two ends of the rope to the eyes of the eyebolt (a tautline hitch is handy here).

If you don't want to use the bolts, you can push the ropes themselves through the holes and tie with strong stopper knots.

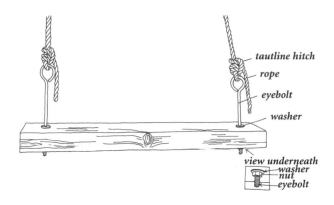

tautline hitch
rope
eyebolt
washer
view underneath
washer
nut
eyebolt

MAKING A PEG BOARD GAME

———————◆———————

Perfect for car journeys or rainy days, this ancient logic game is surprisingly easy to make but difficult to master. Traditionally, it is a triangular board with fourteen pegs and fifteen holes. The goal is to jump one peg over another until only one remains.

What you need

- 1 flat board of wood, 15 centimetres × 15 centimetres (at least one 2 centimetres thick is a good size). Any shape is fine; it doesn't have to be triangular.
- 14 fluted dowel pins, ¾ centimetre × 2 centimetres. Available at any DIY shop.
- Ruler
- Power drill, with a ¾ centimetre bit.

Make a dot at the top of the board for your starting point. Lightly draw one diagonal line and then another, marking your triangle on the wood. In addition to the top dot, mark four dots down one side of the triangle, four along the other side and three dots along the bottom. Draw dots for the middle holes, too. Use your ruler so everything lines up.

You will need help with the next power drilling step.

Drill a 1-centimetre hole right where you have drawn each dot. Some people measure 1 centimetre up the drill bit and put some masking tape on that spot so they can easily gauge the hole, although once you do enough of these, you'll get the feel of it. Test each hole with a dowel, making sure the dowel easily moves in and out. When all fifteen holes are done, shake out the sawdust and you're ready to play.

RULES OF THE GAME: DARTS

———————— ◆ ————————

D ARTS IS ANOTHER GAME with a long history. The game is thought to have been invented by soldiers throwing arrows at the bottom of tree trunks or wooden casks. Modern dartboards are most commonly made of boar bristles or sisal fibres (or, in the case of Velcro dart games, felt). Playing darts takes some practice and some maths skills, but mostly it's just fun to throw something across the room. Make sure you give annoying siblings and small animals a wide berth.

Setting up the board
A regulation board has a diameter of 45 centimetres and is divided by thin metal wire into 22 sections. Make sure to mount your dartboard so that the centre of the double bull (the bull's-eye) is 173 centimetres from the floor. Mark the toeline, called the oche (pronounced to rhyme with 'hockey'), 237 centimetres from the face of the board.

Basic rules
To determine shooting order, each player shoots for the bull's-eye. The one who comes closest gets to go first. Each turn consists of three darts, which must be thrown from behind the oche. For a throw to count, the point of the dart must touch the board. If a dart bounces off the board or misses

it completely, it does not get a score (and also can't be rethrown).

Scoring

The dartboard is divided into wedges, with point values marked along the outer edge of the circle. Two rings overlap the playing area; landing outside these rings scores a player face-value points for that area of the board.

Landing between the first inner ring and the second inner ring scores a player double the points for that section. Landing between the second inner ring and the bull's-eye earns triple points. Hitting outside the outer wire scores nothing.

How to throw

First, aim. Look at the target you want to hit. Lift your arm up, bent at the elbow so that the sharp end of the dart faces the dartboard. The dart should be tipped slightly up. Check your aim and line up the dart with your sight line. Move the hand holding the dart back towards your body, then pitch the dart forward, releasing the dart and making sure to follow through with your arm. The optimal follow-through will end with your hand pointing at the target (not having your hand fall to your side). When throwing, try not to move your body – the throwing action should come from your shoulder.

PLAYING THE GAME: THE 301

The object of this game, which is most commonly played by two people, is to start with a score of 301 and count down to exactly zero. Each player has a three-throw turn, and the point value of their hits is subtracted from 301. A player can only start subtracting once they 'double' – that is, hit one of the doubles on the board. Once that is accomplished, the scores will begin to count. If the total score of the three throws exceeds the remaining score for that player, the score returns to what it was at the start of the turn. A double must be hit to end the game.

PLAYING THE GAME: ROUND THE CLOCK

In this game, players take turns trying to hit each number, from 1 to 20. Each player has a three-throw turn; players advance to the next number on the board by hitting each number in order. The first person to get to 20 wins.

PLAYING THE GAME: CRICKET

This strategy game is typically played with two players, or two teams of two players each. To win at Cricket, a player must 'close' the numbers 15 to 20 and the bull's-eye before any other player, and must also have the highest point count. 'Closing' a number means hitting it three times in one or more turns (hitting a single closes a number in three throws; hitting a double and then a single closes a number in two throws; and hitting a triple closes a number in a single throw). You don't have to close numbers in any particular order – but you do want to close them before the other players.

To keep track of the score, you'll need a scoreboard (a blackboard on the wall or a pen and pad of paper will work). Write out the numbers vertically for each player, from 20 down to 15, then 'B' for bull's-eye. Each player's turn consists of three throws and only darts that land in the numbers 15–20 or in the bull's-eye count. (You don't get points for hitting numbers 1–14.) Points start to accumulate once a number is closed and are tallied as follows: the centre of the bull's-eye is worth 50 points and the outer ring of the bull's-eye gets 25; numbers 15–20 are worth their face value, but landing in the doubles ring doubles the number's value and landing in the triple ring (the inner ring between the doubles ring and the bull's-eye) triples it.

When a player hits a number once, you put a slash (/) by the number. When that number is hit a second time by a player, you turn the slash into an X. When that number is 'closed', or hit a third time, you draw a circle around the X. Once a number has been closed, if any player hits it, the points for that number go to the player who originally closed it. Once a number has been closed by all the players, no points are awarded for that number for the rest of the game. Total up the points after one player closes all her numbers plus the bull's-eye, and the person or team with the highest number of points is the winner.

Darts Lingo

Arrows: Darts

Bust: Hitting a number higher than you need to go out

Chucker: Indifferent thrower

Clock: Dartboard

Double In: Starting a game with a double

Double Out: Winning a game on a double

Hat Trick: Three bull's-eyes

Leg: One game of a match

Slop: Hitting a number other than the one intended

Trombones: A total turn score of 76 points

Wet Feet: Standing with your feet over the line

BIRD WATCHING

———◆———

BIRD WATCHING MIGHT seem difficult (or even boring), but we can assure you it is not. Birds are everywhere – easy to spot and fun to observe. Most birders keep a life-list journal, a kind of bird diary, writing down the birds they see. As you begin to bird, you can use a small spiral notebook to make a life-list journal for yourself, writing down the names of the birds you find, or sketching their distinguishing features so you can look them up in a bird identification book once you're back home. All you need to go bird watching is a pair of binoculars, a good bird guidebook, comfortable clothes, your life-list journal – and some patience. Bird watching demands a certain kind of presence on the part of the birder. You must become a part of nature rather than stand outside it. Here are eight common birds to start you off on a lifetime pursuit of bird watching.

Robin
The robin is a popular bird and a regular visitor to gardens and allotments. It can be seen throughout Europe and is recognizable by its grey-green head and orange underbelly (usually brighter in the male). During the breeding season

female robins build cup-shaped nests, mostly in shrubs and bushes but sometimes in odd places like toilet cisterns or barrels! The robin's song sounds like a whistled musical phrase and can be heard all year round, including at night.

Cool fact:
In the children's story *Babes in the Wood* robins come across the bodies of two children abandoned in the forest and cover them up with leaves to protect them.

Blue Tit

The blue tit is a pretty little bird resident in the UK, which is yellow on the underside with blue wings, tail and cap. They are cheeky birds, not particularly timid, and were among the first birds in the UK to start feeding from domestic bird tables in people's gardens. Their population is on the increase, maybe partly due to their ability to find food all year round, crucial as they don't migrate to warmer countries during winter.

Cool facts:

Baby blue tits are not actually blue; they start life a more yellow colour and become more blue as they grow older. Blue tits are also responsible for pecking into the foil milk bottle caps and drinking the cream from the top of the pint. As less milk is delivered to the door nowadays, they are having to find alternative sources of food.

Birding Tips from Peter Cashwell
(author of *The Verb 'To Bird'*)

1 Get up early. It's good to get outside before sunrise if you want to see and hear birds with the fewest possible distractions (traffic, factory noise, etc.). You can keep birding all day, of course, but the early morning is the best time.

2 Learn a few common birds' appearances well. They give you something to compare to the bird you saw. If you know the robin, you can tell whether this bird was smaller than a robin, or had a whiter belly, or had a thicker bill.

3 Set up a feeder or a birdbath. This brings birds into your garden where you can watch them up close and over a long time. You'll probably also attract several different kinds of birds, which will help you with no.2.

4 Bird with others. More experienced birders can show you all kinds of things you'd probably miss on your own, and most birders like to show less experienced birders the ropes. Even if it's just you and a friend who doesn't know much about birds, two sets of eyes will see more than one (and two sets of field marks will help you figure out what you saw).

5 Bird everywhere. You don't have to be in a national park to see unusual or interesting birds. Some will be at the beach, others in the city park, still others in your garden, and some in that empty plot across the road. Keep looking and you'll see things everywhere.

Common Kingfisher

The common kingfisher is found by water in the UK. It is the only type of kingfisher found here, and it can be identified by its bright, almost metallic blue upper body and orange lower body and its quick, almost whirring way of flying. It catches its food from the water by perching on sticks protruding from the surface, and its main diet consists of small fish and insects.

Cool fact:

When feeding, the common kingfisher plunges and dives into the water, sometimes submerging entirely to catch its prey.

BIRD WATCHING

Kestrel

Kestrels are the commonest bird of prey in the UK. They are large birds with a wing span of around 70–80 centimetres. They tend to hover around 20 metres off the ground, on the look-out for prey. They are not choosy about what they eat and are capable of catching and killing small mammals such as voles and other smaller birds. Their strong eyesight enables them to spot prey from a distance before swooping in for the kill.

Cool fact:

Kestrels sometimes catch their prey and save it for later, to ensure that they don't find themselves without food later in the day. They need to eat around six to eight voles a day to keep them in good condition.

Mallard

The mallard is the most common duck in the UK, and it is said that all other ducks are descended from it. The male has a distinctive green head and grey body, and the female is a drabber brown colour. You'll find them everywhere from local duck ponds to rivers and lakes, and you have almost certainly fed them bread at least once. Mallard ducklings are yellow and brown and can often be seen following the mother mallard in a line.

Cool fact:

When mallards dip their heads into the water, leaving their tails sticking up, they are looking for food under the surface of the water. This movement is called 'dabbling'; drop that into your conversation to impress your friends!

Mute Swan

This is the official name for the birds we usually just refer to as swans. Mute swans are large white birds that live on rivers and lakes. Many people believe that they pair for life, but this is not always the case. They are incredibly loyal to their mate and can be aggressive when defending them. Britain's heaviest birds, they can weigh up to 15 kilos.

Cool fact:

It is a widely known fact that the Queen owns all the swans in England. This is not actually true: she owns all except those owned by the Dyers and Vintners – two livery companies of the City of London.

Tawny Owl

The tawny owl is the commonest owl in the UK. It is a nocturnal bird, which means that you will have to get out and about at night if you are ever to catch a glimpse of it. You have most likely heard its distinctive 'twit twoo' call, but did you know that the 'twit' is the male and the 'twoo' is the female? We didn't make that up, honestly!

Cool fact:
The tawny owl may look sweet, but don't get too close to it as it can be fierce in defending its nest and young. Humans have been injured and even killed by tawny owls.

And now, a birding poem to inspire you:

A Bird Came Down the Walk
by Emily Dickinson

A Bird came down the Walk –
He did not know I saw –
He bit an angle-worm in halves
And ate the fellow, raw.

And then he drank a Dew
From a convenient Grass
And then hopped sidewise to the Wall
To let a Beetle pass –

He glanced with rapid eyes
That hurried all abroad –
They looked like frightened Beads,
    I thought –
He stirred his velvet head

Like one in danger, Cautious,
I offered him a Crumb,
And he unrolled his feathers
And rowed him softer home –

Than Oars divide the Ocean
Too silver for a seam –
Or Butterflies, off Banks of Noon,
Leap, plashless as they swim.

WASHING THE CAR

❖

Y OU CAN FORGO expensive non-eco-friendly shop-bought cleaners for our two wonder products instead.

Before you start washing, sprinkle baking soda through the car's interior to remove odours. Vacuum it up when the outside washing is done.

For the car body, grab a bucket, and pour in 100 millilitres of vinegar for every four litres of water; scrub car with a big sponge.

For windows, mirrors and interior plastic, mix 400 millilitres of water and 100 millilitres of vinegar in an empty spray bottle. You can add up to 50 millilitres of rubbing alcohol and, to make it look fancier, one drop each, no more, of blue and green food colouring. Instead of rags, use newspapers to clean and shine windows.

HOW TO WHISTLE WITH
TWO FINGERS

---◆---

MAKE A TRIANGLE by putting the tips of your little fingers together, palms and fingers facing towards you. Stick out your tongue and put your little fingers right on the centre of it, pushing your tongue strongly against your fingers where they meet. Push your tongue back into your mouth with your fingers, so that your little fingers are inside your mouth up to the first knuckles. Angle your finger-tips slightly down, just behind your bottom teeth and keep your tongue pressing into your fingers. Purse your lips and blow. You may have to adjust the angle of your fingers to get that sound right, but just practise and before you know it you'll be hailing cabs with your piercing two-finger whistle!

LEMON-POWERED CLOCK

◆

A PAIR OF LEMONS and a quick trip to the DIY shop is all you need to convert natural chemical energy into electric power.

Alessandro Volta invented the battery in Italy, in 1800, combining zinc, copper and an acid to create energy. A common lemon can provide acid (as do potatoes, which you

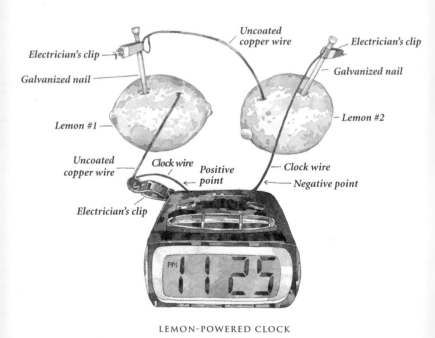

LEMON-POWERED CLOCK

can use if there's no lemon around), and you can rig one to run your own digital clock.

WHAT YOU NEED

1 A battery-operated digital clock without a plug. It can use two AA batteries, or a round battery. Depending on the connections, you have to rig the wires in different ways, but that's where the fun starts.

2 Two fairly large galvanized nails. Nails are measured in length and in diameter (with designations of 3d, 6d, 8d, 10d, and the like). We used a 16d, 3½-inch solid nail. Galvanized nails are a must and we'll explain why below.

3 Copper wire. Uncoated wire is easier. If your wire comes with a coating, use a wire stripper to remove an inch or two of the covering.

4 Three electrician's clips.

5 Two lemons, or one very large lemon, cut in half.

WHAT YOU DO

In five simple steps, here is how you run a digital clock on a lemon.

Step One
Place the lemons on a plate, or any flat surface that can serve as the base for the clock. Push one nail into each lemon and then, as far away from the nails as possible, also push in a strand of copper wire. Label your lemons one and two. What you're going to do now is create a closed circuit, so energy can flow from the lemon into the clock and back again.

Step Two
Open up the clock's battery compartment. Depending on your clock, there are two AA batteries, or a single battery that looks like a button. Remove the battery (you'll be replacing its energy, believe it or not, with the lemon, nail and copper concoction you've just created). Notice that the positive and negative points are marked as such.

Step Three
On lemon number one, use the electrician's clip to connect the copper wire to the positive point in the clock. This may be a challenge; in some cases it is easier said than done.

If you can't connect your wire to the positive point in the battery compartment, you'll need to remove the clock's plastic backing and open up the clock. An adult should help with this, and remember, once you take the clock apart it may not go back together. You'll see that the positive and negative points are connected to wires on the inside of the clock. You can remove the wires from the back of the battery compartment, and then use them to make your connections. If you have a two-AA-battery clock, and inside you find two positive wires, make sure you connect your copper wire with both. Once you've figured this out, the rest is a breeze.

Step Four

On lemon number two, connect the nail to the clock's negative point. You may need to move the lemon into a new position so you can clip the nail to the clock.

Step Five

Link the copper wire from lemon number two to the nail sticking out of lemon number one. You'll see now that you've made an entire electrical circuit, from clock to lemon to the next lemon, and back to the clock. If all has gone well, the clock now works, because just under one volt of electricity is coursing around the circuit.

If the clock does not work, make sure all connections are secure, and then double-check the directions. If several months from now the clock stops, replace the lemons, or the nails, and it should begin ticking once again.

WHY IT WORKS

1 The nail has been galvanized, which means it was coated with zinc to help resist rust. The lemon contains acid. This acid dissolves the zinc on the nail. In chemistry terms, this means that the zinc loses an electron and becomes a positive force. (If you haven't already read the chapter about the Periodic Table of the Elements in the original *Daring Book for Girls*, now's a good time to do so.) The moisture in the lemon functions as an electrolyte, a fluid that conducts electrons – if you will, a swimming pool for electrons.

2 The electron shoots out of the zinc, through the lemon, to react with the copper on the wire. The copper gains an electron and becomes a negative force. The exchange of electrons is a chemical reaction. It creates chemical energy, or charge. All that charge needs is a circuit.

3 The electron exchange buzzes around the circuit you built – zinc/nail to copper wire to clock to copper wire to nail to lemon to copper to zinc/nail to lemon, and so on. That's the transfer from chemical energy to electricity, and it gets the clock going as well as any manufactured battery.

CYCLING

❖

CYCLING IS A GREAT WAY to get out and about, and it's good for you and the environment too. Before you set off, make sure your bicycle is in good working order, your tyres are pumped up and puncture-free, your chain oiled, and your brakes nice and tight. A few more things to remember:

* Always wear a helmet. It will protect your head should you come off your bike.

* Always follow the Highway Code when cycling on the roads. This means stopping at all traffic lights and not cycling on the pavement.

* Always make sure you have lights on you in case it becomes dark while you are out, and make sure they have working batteries too. Reflective strips are also a good idea.

If you follow these simple rules, you'll have fun and will keep safe too.

GREAT DAYS OUT BY BIKE

These are just a few ideas. If you are inspired and would like to find out more, visit www.sustrans.org.uk which has routes for cyclists of all abilities in all areas of the country.

The Great North Way

This is a route of 32 miles that takes you out of North London into Hertfordshire along cycle-friendly roads. The route is clearly marked along the way – just follow the 'Route 12' signs.

Start by taking the train to Hadley Wood train station. The first location you are heading towards is Welham Green, so take a left out of Hadley Wood towards Ganwick Corner. Then follow the road to Dancers Hill and you'll already feel as though you are in the countryside, even though you are close to the M25 and A1. Here you'll even go under the M25, and then you need to follow Mymmshall Brook towards Water End. Then a little way on you'll get to Welham Green. Time to stop for a well-deserved ice-cream.

Next stop on the route is Codicote. Follow Traveller's Lane towards Stream Woods and Howe Dell where you'll go through the secluded woods on the outskirts of Old Hatfield. Continue up Mill Green Lane towards Welwyn Garden City and then take a left onto Turnmill Dale, leading to Ayot Green and Ayot St Peter. After stopping to see the church of Ayot St Peter, take the St Albans Road towards Codicote, mentioned in the Domesday Book. It's probably time for a swift break for sandwiches around here too.

Don't stop too long; you still have a way to go yet. Take Slip Lane towards Old Knebworth, passing Knebworth House and then heading on to Stevenage. Take the Gunnelswood Road and then the Hitchin Road and you'll emerge to the north-east of Stevenage. Ahead is Willian with its famous arboretum, and then Letchworth. This is a lovely market town; you can stop here or, if you are feeling energetic, continue on to Baldock, one of the oldest towns in the county of Hertfordshire. It's up to you now: either catch a train back or cycle back to Hadley Wood.

Pottering around the Cotswolds

This is a shorter route that runs through pretty Cotswolds villages.

Start by taking the train to Moreton-in-Marsh. From here you need to turn left onto the A429 towards Stretton-on-Foss. You'll only need to stay on this road a few miles, so keep an eye out for the turning to Aston Magna on the left. Once on this road you'll be deep in the countryside, surrounded by fields. At Aston Magna take the first right towards Paxton. This is a rough track and one with a couple of hills but it is worth the effort once you arrive in the pretty village of

Paxford. Here is a good place to stop for some lunch. After lunch, keep going along a road called The Cam and you'll get to Chipping Campden.

Chipping Campden is a lovely place to stop for an ice-cream. From here, take the road to Broad Campden, then Draycott, and then on to Batsford. From here you'll have a long, easy, downhill ride all the way back to where you started, just in time to get the train back home.

A stately cycle ride in Yorkshire

This ride is easy and fun, all along flat roads and paths. It takes you from York to Beningbrough Hall following cycle route 65.

Start in York by the River Ouse at Lendall Bridge. The first part of the route follows the river and is on traffic-free cycle paths. Then follow the signs to Overton and then Shipton where you'll go through the pretty villages on a quiet country lane. From Shipton follow the signs to Beningbrough Hall. The hall is a stately home that is well worth a visit in itself. A grand Georgian house, it is filled with impressive paintings and surrounded by a magnificent walled garden. To get back to York from Beningbrough, simply retrace your route the way you came.

Canal life in Scotland

This is an easy and picturesque ride along one of Scotland's greatest canals.

Start at the canal centre in Linlithgow, dropping in at the museum to find out more about the canal you'll be cycling along. Take the cycle path west (following signs for cycle route 76). And that's it! The route is entirely straight along the canal so you'll be able to concentrate on seeing Scotland's longest waterway tunnel, the Avon Aqueduct, marvelling at the length of this canal, which is uninterrupted by locks – a first at the time it was built. The route ends at Falkirk where you can see the Falkirk wheel, the only rotating boat lift in the world.

TAKING CARE OF YOUR BIKE

A daring girl should be able to take care of her own bicycle, so here are a few tips on what to do if your bike goes wrong.

How to mend a puncture

However lucky you are and however good your tyres are, you'll get a puncture at least once in your cycling life. Hopefully it will be somewhere close to home, but you should be prepared and able to fix the puncture at the side of the road if necessary.

* First let all the air out of your inner tube so you can take the tyre off the wheel. Tyre levers can help you here.

* Then take the inner tube off the wheel. You'll need to find the hole, and the best way to do this is to pump the inner tube up and then hold it underwater and look for the bubbles that indicate where air is escaping. If you are on the road this is trickier and you may just have to listen for the sounds of air escaping.

* Having found the hole, mark it with a piece of chalk so you don't lose it again.

* Your puncture repair kit should have a slightly abrasive section on the outside of the case; use this gently to rough up the area around the hole – it will help the patch stick.

* Cover the area around the hole with glue and leave for a few minutes to go tacky.

* Then cover with a patch and hold down for a couple of minutes to make sure it sticks.

* Then you need to put the inner tube back into the tyre (inflating it slightly before you put it in the tyre will make sure you don't trap it or kink it under the tyre). Then place the tyre and inner tube back onto the wheel. You'll notice an arrow on the tyre – make sure that this is pointing in the direction that the wheel rotates.

* Finally, using the tyre levers again, attach the tyre to the wheel rim and pump up the inner tube once more.

It's a bit of a messy job but one that is very satisfying to be able to do yourself, and it gets easier with practice.

Tightening your brakes

Good brakes are vital to your safety as a cyclist, so it is important that you keep them in working order. You don't want to regret not knowing how to do this.

* Loosen the cable clamp bolt. You'll find this next to your brake levers on your handlebars – the brake cable comes out of it.

* Pull the brake cable through very slightly to tighten the brakes.

* Screw the cable clamp bolt up again.

* Check that your brakes are tighter and more responsive, and always take care the first few times you use your brakes after tightening them – they'll react faster so you may skid if you are not careful.

While you are tightening your brakes, check that your brake blocks are not worn down. You'll need to replace them every six months or so (depending on how often you cycle) so keep an eye on them and go to a bicycle repair shop when they need replacing.

Lights

Before you go out, especially in winter, make sure your lights are working properly. You need a white front light and a red rear light at the very least. You want to be seen by the traffic at all times. Rechargeable batteries are good, but remember to charge them up regularly.

HOW TO BE A SPY

❖

THE WORD 'SPY' comes to us from ancient words meaning 'to look at' or 'to watch'. And indeed, despite the modern movie emphasis on technology and machines as integral to a spy's bag of tricks, in essence what makes an excellent spy is her ability to watch, pay attention, look and learn.

TOP-SECRET COMMUNICATION

Girl Guide whistles and hand signals

These secret signals have been used by the Girl Guides since before World War I. You can use them to alert or direct your spy team when you are out in the field.

Whistle signals

* One long blast means 'silence/alert/listen for next signal'

* A succession of long slow blasts means 'go out/get further away' or 'advance/extend/scatter'

- A succession of quick short blasts means 'rally/close in/come together/fall in'

- Alternate short and long blasts mean 'alarm/look out/ be ready/man your alarm posts'

Hand signals

- Advance/forward: Swing the arm from rear to front, below the shoulder

- Retreat: Circle the arm above the head

- Halt: Raise the arm to full extension above the head

Secret codes

A code is a way to send a message while keeping it a secret from someone who isn't supposed to know about it. Codes can be easy or complicated – the trick is to make sure the person on the receiving end of your secret message has the key to decode it without making it too easy for anyone else to crack. Here are a few simple codes you can use.

* Write each word backwards

* Read every second letter

* Use numbers for letters (A=1, B=2, C=3, etc.)

* Reverse the alphabet (A=Z, B=Y, C=X, etc.)

* Sliding scale alphabet (move the alphabet by one letter: A=B, B=C, C=D, etc.)

* Use invisible ink (write with lemon or lime juice; after it dries hold the paper up to a light source to read the message)

* Pigpen code: Each letter is represented by the part of the 'pigpen' that surrounds it in the key. If it's the second letter in the box, then it has a dot in the middle.

Key

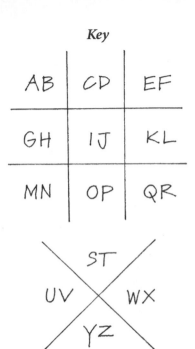

Code

∨⊓⊓⨀ ∨⊔⊓⨀⌐∨!

TOP SECRET!

HOW TO BE A SPY

TOOLS

In films, spies often use high-tech equipment to accomplish covert tasks, but all spies are grounded in the basics: good, old-fashioned, low-tech observation that can be performed without the aid of any fancy technology. In World War II, women spies used something called an 'escape and evasion' scarf – these were scarves with maps printed on one side, so that any agent who needed to find an escape route or nearby town or road had a map that was easy to get to but not so easily detectable by someone else. You can make your own with an old scarf or other fabric and a permanent marker (providing you get permission to mark up the scarf first).

A few other tools that would be good for a spy to have handy are things like binoculars; a small notepad and pen; walkie-talkie; magnifying glass; Swiss Army knife; hat or wig for quick disguising; plimsolls or other quiet shoes for stealth walking; clothes in dark or subdued colours. The best tools of all, though, are your eyes, your ears and your ingenuity. Pay attention to everything that's going on around you, blend into your surroundings so you can observe without being noticed, look for subtle clues to tell you more about what's happening and write everything down. With any luck, you'll not only become a great spy, you'll be on your way to becoming a great writer. You know, just in case the espionage career doesn't work out.

YOUR SPY TEAM

The life of a spy can be a lonely one, with so much secrecy and subterfuge and no one to share it with at the risk of blowing your cover. It's much more fun to operate within a spy ring and work as a team to accomplish your undercover goals. On a team, spies can have specific tasks or areas of expertise, and of course code names.

The Agent-in-Charge: This is the head spy. She is responsible for directing, planning and organizing the mission. All team members report to her.

The Scout: This is the person who scopes out the physical landscape to see if it's safe for the rest of the team to move in. She goes ahead of the team when they are out in the field and no one moves in without a signal from her. She should have excellent eyesight and hearing and should be an expert on geography and the outdoors.

The Tracker: This person acts as the 'trigger', the spy whose job it is to monitor the target of investigation. She tracks and observes the suspect's actions and alerts the rest of the team when the suspect is in range.

The Techie: This is the group's technology maven. She knows about computers, tools and gadgets, from using them to fixing them to creating new ones. She is the one who draws up any maps, plans or charts, and also keeps notes about the mission.

The Wheel Artist: This is the person who organizes the getaway, or who can use her wheels to accomplish any stealth manoeuvre. If she can drive, that's great, but she doesn't have to be commandeering a car. The wheels can be anything that gets your spy team out of the field in a timely manner. She can oversee a fleet of scooters, ride another spy to safety on her bike or even accomplish a sensitive mission lightning quick on her skateboard or roller skates.

The Stealth Master: This is a small, quiet person who can sneak into tight places and generally move around unnoticed. It helps if she is also a master of disguise and an illusionist, able to use card and magic tricks for purposes of distraction.

The Social Engineer: This person is brave, chatty, outgoing and able to interact with suspects and others to extract information. She can be the public face of the team while other team members gather evidence or perform surveillance, using her considerable social skills both to distract and engage.

Of course, no matter what her speciality, a spy should be able to: appraise a situation, balance, bluff, climb, be diplomatic, escape when necessary, gather information, hide, intuit, be insightful, jump, listen, move silently, read lips and body language, respond quickly, tumble, transform and, above all, be level-headed.

After each mission, all members of the spy team should rendezvous at an agreed-upon meeting place or secret hideout, where they will report to the agent-in-charge and exchange information. No matter what her role on the team is, a spy should always note suspicious activity, try not to be seen or heard, cover her tracks and never reveal her true identity to outsiders.

Acorn
Someone who is performing an intelligence function.

Agent
A person officially employed by an intelligence service. (Also undercover agent: *a secret agent;* deep-cover agent: *an agent under permanent cover;* double agent: *an agent simultaneously working for two enemies;* agent-in-charge: *the head agent.)*

Babysitter
Bodyguard.

Blowback
Unexpected negative consequences of spying.

Blown
Detected, as in 'your cover is blown'.

Bona Fides
Proof of a person's claimed identity.

Brush Contact or Brush Pass
Brief contact between two agents who are passing information, documents or equipment.

Burn Notice
An official statement from an intelligence agency saying that an individual or group is an unreliable source.

Chicken Feed
Low-grade information given by a double agent to an adversary to build the credibility of the double agent.

Cobbler
Spy who creates false passports, visas, certificates and other documents.

Comm
Small note or other written communication.

Cover
A secret identity.

Dead Drop
A secret hiding place somewhere in public where communications, documents or equipment are placed for another agent to collect.

Doppelgänger
A decoy or lookalike.

E&E
Escape and evasion.

Ears Only
Material too secret to commit to writing.

Eyes Only
Documents too secret to be talked about.

Floater
A person used occasionally or even unknowingly for an intelligence operation.

Friend
An agent or informant providing information.

Front
A legitimate-appearing business created to provide cover for spies and their operations.

Ghoul
Agent who searches obituaries and graveyards for names to be used by agents.

Honey Pot/Honey Trap
Slang for use of men or women to trap a person using affection or romance.

Informant
A person who provides intelligence to the surveillance team.

Joe
A deep-cover agent.

Legend
Background story or documents to support your cover.

Letterbox
A person who acts as a go-between.

Mole
An agent who penetrates enemy organizations.

Naked
A spy operating without cover or backup.

Paroles
Passwords agents use to identify each other.

Peep
Photographer.

Pocket Litter
Items in a spy's pocket (receipts, coins, etc.) that add authenticity to her identity.

Ring
A network of spies or agents.

Safe House
A secret hideout.

Sanitize
To 'clean up' a report or other document to hide sensitive information.

Sleeper Agents
Spies who are placed in a target country or organization, not to undertake an immediate mission, but to be activated later.

Spook
Another word for spy.

Target
The person being spied on. (Also hard target: A target who actively maintains secrecy and doesn't let on that she is aware of the surveillance team.)

The Take
Information gathered by spying.

Trigger
An agent who watches for the target and alerts the rest of the surveillance team when the target is spotted.

Unsub
An unknown subject in a surveillance operation.

Undercover
Disguising your identity, or using an assumed identity, in order to learn secret information.

Window Dressing
Like pocket litter, this is extra information included in a cover story to help make it seem more real.

FIVE KARATE MOVES

◆

KARATE BEGAN IN THE FIFTH CENTURY BC as a set of mind-strengthening exercises. Legend says that it was brought to a small forest temple in China by a Zen Buddhist monk named Bodhidharma (Bo-dee-darma) who, amazingly, had walked there all the way from India. Below are five basic moves that are fun to do with friends. To learn more and to take karate more seriously, look for a professional teacher in this and other martial arts.

Front Kick

The front kick is Karate's most powerful kick. Bring your left knee up to waist level, then extend the rest of the leg

Front Kick

straight out. Your right leg should be firmly grounded to balance the kick, and your arms should be held close to your chest. Try the quick-surprise front kick, and then try a slower but more forceful variation.

Back Kick

Stand in a comfortable position facing forward. Your right leg is your kicking leg. Bend your left non-kicking leg just a little bit to give your body extra support and balance. Look over your right shoulder. Find your target. Bend your right knee, aim your heel in a straight line towards your target and kick

Back Kick

your foot high behind you. Your eyes are very important in this kick. Keep looking at your target while you kick back, extending your leg. Pull your leg back in the same path you used for your kick. Alternate kicking leg.

Punch and Pull

Face forward with your feet shoulder-width apart. Keeping your right leg straight, lunge forward with your left leg, bending at the knee. Push your right arm forward

Punch and Pull

in front of your body, with your hand in a downward-facing fist. Your left arm stays back, at your side, with your left hand in an upward-facing fist. Now, punch forward with the left arm and twist the wrist so that when this arm fully extends, your fist faces down. While the left arm punches, the right arm comes to rest at your side, with hand in an upward-facing fist. Alternate punches.

Knife Hand, or Classic Karate Chop

Open your hand and turn it so your thumb faces the ceiling and your little finger faces the floor. Extend your fingers

Knife Hand

FIVE KARATE MOVES

forward and away from you. The fingers should lightly touch. Let your thumb fall into the palm of your hand, and bend the top of the thumb downwards. Arch the hand slightly backwards. Raise your hand above your shoulder. Swing diagonally downwards across to the other side of your body aiming to strike your target with the part of your hand that's just below your little finger.

Lunge Punch

Face forward, with your feet shoulder-width apart. Place your left leg in front of the right, and bend your knee into a lunge.

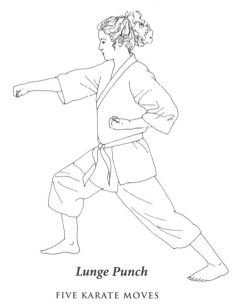

Lunge Punch

FIVE KARATE MOVES

Keep your right leg straight. This is called front stance. Step forward with your right foot into a powerful lunge, and as your right foot lands, punch forward with the right hand. To add power, at the same time as you punch the right fist forward, pull your left hand back to your left side in an upward-facing fist. Pull your punching hand back to lunge again, alternating sides, or to change to another move.

ESSENTIAL GEAR

───◆───

1 **Swiss Army Knife.** A key tool for survival, exploring and camping, it's a knife, screwdriver and saw with loads of extras like a magnifying glass, nail file, bottle opener, scissors and tweezers. Best of all it fits in your pocket. Clean with hot soapy water and add a tiny drop of mechanical oil once every three blue moons.

2 **Bandana.** Can be used to keep your head cool, protect your belongings, wrap a present. Tied to a stick, it can carry your treasured possessions on your adventures.

3 **Rope and String.** A stretch of rope and a knowledge of knots will take you many places – and may also help get you out of them.

4 **Notepad and Pencil, with a Back-up Pen.** Life is about memories: a quick sketch of a bird or plant, a wish list, a jot of the most important thought ever. A pad and pencil is also perfect for spying or for writing.

5 **Hair Band.** For when hair gets in the way. At a pinch, you can also use your bandana or a pencil.

6 **Bungee Strap.** For strapping things down on the go.

7 **Torch.** Basic tool for camping and reading under the covers late at night. A small piece of red Cellophane over the lens makes ghost stories even creepier. Eventually you can graduate to a headlamp, so your hands are free.

8 **Compass.** You need to know where you are and a compass can help. Hang it around your neck along with a whistle.

9 **Safety Pins.** Because they're good to have on hand when things need to be put back together, or when you want to express eternal friendship to a new friend by decorating with a few beads as a gift.

10 **Gaffer Tape.** Two inches wide and hard as nails. It can fix almost everything. Good for treehouse construction.

11 **Deck of Cards and a Good Book.** Old standbys.

12 Patience. It's a quality and not a thing, but it's essential so we'll include it here. Forget perfect on the first try. In the face of frustration, your best tool is a few deep breaths, and remembering that you can do anything once you've practised two hundred times. Seriously.

MISCELLANEA

◆

If you have yet to exhaust the possibilities of a languid day, here are more things to do, in no particular order.

1 **Skip Stones.** Find a rock as smooth, flat and round as possible. Hold it flattest-side down, index finger curled around one edge and throw it sidearm, low and parallel to the water, snapping the wrist at the last possible moment before you let go to give it some spin. The stone should hit the water at a low, 20 degree angle or so. Keep practising till the stone bounces off the water a few times.

2 **Go Sledging.** Find a hill with virgin snow as yet untouched by other daring girls (you'll have to get up early to find this!). Drag your sledge to the top and enjoy the ride. An important note on steering a sledge: it's opposite to how you steer a bicycle or a car and akin to a kayak or canoe. Lean left to go right. Lean right to go left.

3 **Throw Water Balloons.** To fill, attach the mouth of the balloon to the tap (or use an adapter that comes with many packages of water balloons) and – this is key – keep the tap on low so the water pressure doesn't send the balloon into

outer space. Once the water balloon smashes to the ground, clean up the colourful scraps, since when the fun's over, the balloon remnants turn into rubbish.

4 **Play Ping-Pong.** Forget nudging your parents for a horse; ask for a ping-pong table instead. Have a good supply of those air-filled white balls ready for when they lodge in the crevices between storage boxes that have been stacked high against the cellar walls to make space for the ping-pong table. If you're alone you can fold one of the table sides to vertical and push it against a wall to practise.

5 **Play the Harmonica.** Invaluable for nights by the campfire when the embers are low, the camp songs are over and nearly everyone has fallen asleep. Hold the harmonica with your thumb and first finger. Blow breath into it and draw it back through the holes. Experiment with sound. Flapping the other fingers up and down while you blow or draw will create a wavery vibrato.

6 **Pop a Wheelie.** Whether yours is a tough mountain bike or a ladylike pastel blue number with tassels on the handlebars and a basket, you'll want to know how to pop a wheelie. Once you're at speed, lean forward, hands grabbing the handlebars and then shift your body weight slightly up

and backwards. That should be enough to lift the front wheel off the ground, whether you're doing show-offs on the street in front of your house, or trying to get your bike over tree stumps on a rugged trail.

7 **Play Handball.** Find a clean wall with no windows or another flat surface and bounce a rubber ball against it, open-handed. It's the best way possible to discover what your hands can do and to learn about angles of reflection. Play alone or with friends rotating in when someone misses the ball.

8 **Take Things Apart.** Old televisions and fax machines, a mobile phone that no longer works or a computer that's ten years out of date and living its final years in the garden shed: no discarded machine should go undismantled. Teensy-tiny drivers and hex keys can unlock the smallest screws, so grab a hammer and whatever does the trick and see what's inside. That's how the world's best engineers learned what they know.

9 **Make a Memory Box.** This girlhood of yours is filled with days to remember. Make a scrapbook if you like, but really, any old box will do. Keep your mementos, letters, ticket stubs, the list of dreams scribbled on a napkin, a picture of

your best friends and the poem or phrase you thought up last night before bed. Stow this box of inspiration somewhere safe, keep adding to it and don't look at it for twenty years.

10 **Whittle.** Put that Swiss Army knife to good use. With the knife in one hand and the wood in the other, shave off the bark and whittle away at fallen branches. No other directions are necessary; as you start trimming, the wood will begin to take shape and you'll know when you're done. Keep the knife sharp (a whetstone comes in handy) and cut away from your body, hands and fingers and away from anyone or thing that can get hurt.

11 **Climb a Tree.** Any tree. The trick is to push your legs and the plane of your body diagonally against the tree while your arms reach around the trunk. That way, you aren't trying to defy gravity entirely. Shimmy up the trunk this way bit by bit until you reach the branches and then head for the sky.

12 **Read Aloud.** Summer afternoons are made for reading out loud to your family and friends. Sentences have rhythms that come alive with the sound of your voice. Act out the parts if you wish or make up a play from the book's characters or your own.

13 **Go on a Scavenger Hunt.** Outdoors: one person makes a list of things likely to be found in your backgarden or local park. Then everyone else goes off on the hunt to find as many of those things as possible. The person who finds the most on her list wins! Indoors: find items in the house beginning with each letter of the alphabet in order from A to Z. Or create a trail of clues to one ultimate 'treasure' that your scavengers can discover.

ADVENTURES & PURSUITS

The DARING Book for Girls

Andrea Buchanan and Miriam Peskowitz

Andrea Buchanan and Miriam Peskowitz

The Pocket

DARING

Book

for

Girls

Discoveries & Pastimes

ILLUSTRATIONS

Illustrations on pp 1, 4, 7, 12, 15, 19, 24–7, 29–32, 34, 36, 44, 48, 57, 61, 63–9, 78–9, 84–5, 102–4, 106–7, 109, 113, 128–9, 144, 146, 148, 164, 166, 184, 195–9 © Alexis Seabrook

Illustrations on pp i, 16, 70–2, 80–2, 116–7, 119, 121, 141 © Joy Gosney